THE DEATH OF LIFE

Seán McDonagh

The Death of Life:
The Horror of Extinction

the columba press

First published in 2004 by
the columba press
55A Spruce Avenue, Stillorgan Industrial Park,
Blackrock, Co Dublin

Cover by Bill Bolger
Origination by The Columba Press
Printed in Ireland by ColourBooks Ltd, Dublin

ISBN 1 85607 464 1

Acknowledgements

The poem 'The One' by Patrick Kavanagh is reproduced with the permission of the Trustees of the Estate of the late Katherine B. Kavanagh, through the Jonathan Williams Literary Agency.

I would like to thank my colleagues here at St Columban's, Dalgan Park – Frs Oliver Kennedy, Patrick Conneally, Neil Collins, Pat Connaughton, Michael Duffy, Pat Raleigh, Noel Lynch and Tom O'Reilly – for encouragement and support while writing this book.

I am dedicating the book to Fr Cyril Hally. He arrived in Ireland in 1963 and immediately opened up a new world of cultural anthropology and mission studies for my generation of missionaries. For me, and many others, he has been an inspiration and guiding figure. His years at the Pacific Mission Institute in Sydney were particularly fruitful for the church in Oceania. As director of the institute in the early 1980s he encouraged me to teach a course in creation theology. This was probably one of the first Catholic institutions to host such a course.

For Fr Cyril T. Hally
priest, missiologist, gardener, mentor,
friend and fellow-Columban missionary

Table of Contents

List of Abbreviations

CDB	Convention on Biodiversity
CIDSE	International Cooperation for Development and Solidarity
CITES	Convention on International Trade in Endangered Species
FAO	United Nations Food and Agriculture Organisation
FSC	Forest Stewardship Council
GATT	The General Agreement on Tariffs and Trade
IPCC	Irish Peatland Conservation Council
IPCC	Intergovernmental Panel on Climate Change
IUCN	International Union for the Conservation of Nature
IWMI	International Water Management Institute
MTAs	Material Transfer Agreements
OPW	Office of Public Works
RSPB	Royal Society for the Protection of Birds
SAC	Special Areas of Conservation
SAPs	Structural Adjustment Programmes
WWF	Word Wide Fund for Nature

CHAPTER ONE

Introduction

The wealth of the world, if measured by domestic product and per-capita consumption, is rising. But if calculated from the condition of the biosphere, it is falling.
— Edward O. Wilson, *The Future of Life*, 2002

Most scientists and well-informed people worldwide now acknowledge that human activity has altered, in a substantial way, the living systems of planet Earth, especially in recent decades. The catalogue of environmental destruction is extensive and, unfortunately, often irreversible. Humans are polluting air, water and soils and promoting the extinction of many of the creatures who have been our companions on the planet for millions of years. The dangers associated with major climatic changes stemming from global warming, especially the damage caused by super-storms, are now being taken seriously by actuaries in the insurance industry and even by the film industry. *The Day after Tomorrow*, released in May 2004, employed all the special effects techniques of Hollywood to illustrate how global warming might cause the Gulf Stream to stop flowing in the North Atlantic thus triggering a new ice age.

After President George W. Bush signalled that he would not abide by the Kyoto Agreement on Climate Change in March 2001, the renowned Harvard biologist, Edward O. Wilson, joined other academics in writing 'A Letter to President Bush', *Time* (9 April, 2001), pleading with him to 'reduce US production of greenhouse gases'. Wilson is obviously concerned about global warming but he considers that the 'quenching of life's exuberance will be more consequential to humanity than all of present-day global warming, ozone depletion and pollution combined'.[1]

A decade earlier Professor Wilson wrote the book *The*

---

1. Edward O. Wilson, 'Vanishing Before Our Eyes', *Time Special Edition*, April/May 2000, page 30.

Diversity of Life. In it he estimated that 27,000 species were being lost each year.[2] Many experts now consider this to be quite a conservative estimate. Wilson warned, however, that the destruction of species would soar as the last remaining areas of tropical forests are exploited and destroyed. The British scientist, Sir Robert May, believes that species are now perishing at 1,000 or even 10,000 times the 'background' extinction over the past 600 million years.[3] As a result, the World Conservation Union's 2002 Red List (list of endangered species) contained 11,167 species of plants and animals.[4] But tens of thousands more are endangered.

In the course of a documentary on the extinction of species, entitled *State of the Planet*, screened on BBC 1 on 29 November 2000, David Attenborough said that unless major protective measures are taken now we could lose up to half of the species of our world in the next 50 to 100 years. The possibility that human activity could sterilise the planet in such a short period should have sent shock waves, registering about eight on the Richter scale, right around the world. It should have rallied governments, corporations, religions and citizens to protect the delicate web of life, since each strand pulled from the closely knit fabric of life endangers the survival of other species, including humans. In fact, I did not see a single comment in the newspapers in Britain and Ireland or hear a word on the electronic media during the following days.

In 2002 the United Nations Environment Programme published a report entitled *Global Environment Outlook*.[5] The report identified 11,046 species of plants and animals that are endangered. These included 1,130 mammals and 1,183 species of birds. The scientists who worked on the report believe that the

---

2. Edward O. Wilson, *The Diversity of Life*, Penguin, London, page 268.
3. Tim Radford, 'Creatures are becoming extinct at a frightening rate. So who cares?' *The Guardian*, 7 April 2000.
4. David Harding, 'The end is near for 121 species', *London Metro Newspaper*, 8 October 2003.
5. *Global Environment Outlook*, Earthscan Publications Ltd, London, pages 120-148.

real figure for organisms facing extinction is probably higher. Even more ominous, they point out that the factors that have given rise to species extinction in recent years, particularly the loss or destruction of habitat, continue to operate with ever-increasing intensity. Unless issues of extinction are faced and properly resourced, it is certain the earth will be a more impoverished place in 30 years' time. Tigers, gorillas, rhinoceros, cheetahs and Asian elephants, to mention just a few, will no longer exist in the wild.

There is a danger that many species will become extinct before they are discovered and classified and their potentially beneficial properties studied. At this point in time there is a shortage of biologists, botanists and taxonomists and there is major underfunding of biology research centres. This is particularly true of Third World countries where there is such richness of biodiversity. The systematic description of species is critical to the preservation of species.

Fr Thomas Berry, an American Passionist priest who has written extensively on the environment, argues that the disruptions to the biosphere are so extensive and irreversible that they constitute changes of a geological and biological order of magnitude. He likens them to the changes which took place at the end of the Mesozoic period (Middle Life) when the dinosaurs became extinct, over 60 million years ago.

My own involvement in biodiversity
My own involvement in environmental issues, especially extinction of species, stemmed from the fact that I was a missionary on the island of Mindanao in the Philippines in the 1970s and 1980s. It would be fair to say that my ecological conversion took a long time and, if I had not been asked to work among a tribal people in the Philippines, it might not have happened at all. My early years as a seminarian or even as a young priest did not point in an environmental direction whatsoever.

My formal missionary education began when I entered the seminary at Dalgan Park, Navan, Co Meath in my late teens in the autumn of 1962. Dalgan is located about four miles on the

Dublin side of Navan in the estate of Dowdstown House. I spent
7 years there studying for the priesthood, surrounded by a variety of native and exotic trees, but paid little attention to them.
The folklore in the area claimed that the various clumps of trees
on the property were planted in the second and third decade of
the 19th century by the then owner, General Taylor. Taylor had
fought alongside Wellington in the Battle of Waterloo. It was
said that the clusters of trees in Dowdstown were sown to mark
the positions taken up by the different British regiments as they
lined up to do battle with Napoleon at Waterloo. Taylor combined 'native' trees like ash, oak, hazel, holly and willow with
horse and Spanish chestnuts and beech with Scots Pine, giant
Californian Redwoods and sturdy Cedars of Lebanon.

Sadly, in the formal classes on philosophy, theology, spirituality or literature I heard very little that might increase my
knowledge of trees or my respect for them. We were not even
encouraged to show the basic courtesy that one creature ought
to show to another by learning its proper name. It was only
when I returned to Dalgan in the 1990s that I noticed the large
Redwoods and the two Cedars of Lebanon. By then I had under-
gone my conversion.

There was one memorable reminder each year. It was that
beautiful, plaintive melody which was sung during the ceremony
of the exaltation of the Cross in the Good Friday Liturgy. As the
minister unveiled the cross, we seminarians and all the Catholic
faithful were asked to sing *Ecce lignum crucis in quo salus mundi
perpendit* ... (Behold the wood of the cross on which hung the
saviour of the world). We answered: *Venite Adoremus* (Come, let
us worship). But the truth is we did not ponder the cross for long
but looked rather to the Christ figure which was nailed to it. This
tendency to discard the natural world in favour of the human
and divine was also very much to the fore in the presentation of
christology. Theology was so overwhelmed by the divinity of
Christ, for most of the last millennium, that any real understanding of the humanity of Christ was almost lost. Needless to say,
classical christology did not locate the humanity of Jesus within

the larger earth-community and cosmic context. The theory of evolution was still very suspect and the text books did not dwell on the fact that, without bacteria, flowers or mammals, no human being, including Jesus, would ever walk on the earth.

When I look back, there was a major lacuna in my theology and spirituality. Over one third of a century later I still find it difficult to reconcile the fact that during those seven years nature was overlooked and forgotten, especially since creation-centred doctrines are at the core of the Catholic faith. These include a belief in God's action in creation, the doctrine of the incarnation which proclaims that God became part of creation, and our belief that we encounter God in a special way in the sacraments which involve created realities like bread, wine, water and oil. It is ironic that Catholics robustly defended a sacramental practice in polemics against the Reformers from the 16th century onwards and still could be blind to what was happening to the natural world. I was never encouraged to explore whether or not the natural world might have any significant role to play in my faith, my spirituality or my understanding of mission. Obviously we did not pay attention to our ancient Irish Christian heritage, including our patron St Columban. In his Sermon, 'Concerning the Faith', Columban writes about the presence of God in nature and the importance of understanding nature if we wish to know God: *Amplius non requiras de Deo; quia volentibus altam scire profunditatem rerum ante natura consideranda est.* (Seek no further concerning God; for those who wish to know the great deep must first review the natural world.) [6] He begins the next paragraph with the exhortation: *Intellege, si vis scire Creatorem, creaturam.* (Understand the creature, if you wish to know the Creator.) [7]

Unfortunately, the situation has hardly changed in many seminaries and theological institutes in the intervening 35 years. Seminaries and theological institutions are more sophisticated

6. *Scriptores Latini Hiberniae,* Volume II, *Sancti Columbani Opera,* ed. G. S. M. Walker, School of Celtic Studies, Dublin Institute for Advanced Studies, 1957, page 65.
7. Ibid., page 65.

today. But, to the best of my knowledge, very few of the theological institutes either in Ireland, Britain, mainland Europe or the US have a significant number of courses on ecology or what is often called 'creation theology' today. Hopefully this will change in the next few years.

To be fair to my mentors in the seminary I did not leave Dalgan empty handed. I had a good education in biblical studies, a new appreciation of the meaning and nature of sacramentality, and the beginnings of an understanding of the importance of culture both in the articulation of faith and in ritual. I was also aware that in the years immediately after Vatican II Catholic theological reflections on God were beginning to move away from viewing God as so absolute, self-sufficient and transcendent that he was unmoved by pain and destruction either in the human or the wide earth-community. From my scripture studies, Catholic social teaching and the documents of the Second Vatican Council, I began to develop a different picture of God. I began to see God as the more caring and sensitive One who is intimately involved with the poor and marginalised. But even that did not extend to experiencing God in the natural world around me.

Even during my first decade as a missionary in the Philippines I was still blind to what was happening to creation. From the time I landed in Mindanao in 1969, I could see how swollen rivers were carrying topsoil down to lagoons and turning them chocolate brown in the wake of a typhoon or a heavy monsoon downpour. Intuitively I knew that this was wrong but I did not understand the full nature of the devastation that was being caused by deforestation. I remember a particular typhoon during 1970 when I was assigned in the coastal city of Oroquieta in North West Mindanao. The swollen river engulfed the homes of poor people close to the river bank. Many people, especially the very young and the elderly, were drowned and the town was devastated. There was huge concern in the parish for the survivors and money, clothes and household goods were collected and made available to help them. Many people knew that the logging on Mount Malindang during the previous three decades was responsible for the flash flood but no one, in public life or within the Catholic Church, was demanding the ending of logging and the replanting of the mountain.

It was not a question of religious leaders being callous and not being interested in the welfare of people. On the contrary, in the late 1960s and early 1970s the energies of Filipino bishops, priests, lay people and of many missionaries like myself were focused on economic, social and equality issues. Concerted efforts were made to help poor communities fight poverty through a variety of small scale income-generating schemes. Others devoted their energies to understanding what factors were causing injustice in the country and especially in the rural areas. Church personnel promoted land reform and worked with farming organisations like the Federation of Free Farmers, to get legal land titles for poor farmers.

After martial law was declared by President Marcos in September 1971, missionaries co-operated with other non-government organisations (NGOs) in protecting the human rights of those who were imprisoned without due process. In those early years I shared the view of many in the social action movement that ecological concerns were more likely to be championed by the upper class, economically secure people who were not engaged in the political or economic struggle. In fact ecological concerns could appear to be a distraction from the pressing work of building a more just and caring society. Subsequent experience proved how wrong I was.

CHAPTER 2

Conversion in the T'boli hills

We are distant cousins to the stars and near relatives to the oceans, plants, and all living creatures on our planet.
— Sally McFague, *The Body of God*, page 104.

My interest in trees and forests really blossomed during the twelve years I spent living with the T'boli people in South Cotabato in the Philippines. The T'boli are a tribal people who live in the diphterocarp forests of Mindanao. There are six kinds of tropical forests in the Philippines – the mangrove forests along the coasts, the beach forests, the molave forests, the diphterocarp forests found in the Cordilleras, Mindoro and Zambales, the Pine forests in higher ground in Luzon, and the mossy forest found above an altitude of 1,000 metres.[1]

The rainforests are a world of beauty, colour, enchantment and fruitfulness. Though they cover only 6% of the land area of the world, at least half and possibly as much as 80% of the world's species live in the rainforests of the world. Many of the drugs found in chemist shops owe their origin to rainforest plants or animals. Unfortunately this has not spared them from the bulldozers and chain-saws of global timber corporations. Between 1990 and 2000 the Food and Agriculture Organisation (FAO) estimated that more than 150 million hectares of tropical forests were converted to other uses. This is about the size of Mexico.[2] At present rates of destruction from logging and burning all the tropical forests of the earth could be gone in 50 to 70 years.

1. *Decline of Philippine Forests*, Environmental Science for Social Change, Inc., 1/F Manila Observatory Bldg, Ateneo de Manila University, Quezon City, Philippines.
2. Donella Meadows, Jorgen Randers, Dennis Meadow, *Limits to Growth: The 30-Year Update*, Chelsea Green Publishing Company, Vermont, 2004, page 76.

Within a few months of arriving in the T'boli hills, I realised how important the forest was in the life of this tribal people. It provided them with building material for their houses and food for them to eat. In the forest they found plants, animals and reptiles that provided them with cures for many diseases. But beyond meeting bodily needs, much of their music, dance, poetry and arts were centred on themes and sounds from the forest. Finally, the forest featured prominently in their religious traditions and rituals.

It became clear to me that, unless the remaining area of the forest was protected, the T'boli, and other tribal groups who lived in the area, would have no future within a period of 30 or 40 years. So one of the major goals of my missionary work for the next 12 years was to help them protect what was left of the forest and replant native species wherever it was possible. That meant learning as much as I could about the rich life of the rainforest from T'bolis themselves and biologists and botanists who were studying the forests. In the T'boli hills I had first-hand experience of some of the processes that cause extinction.

Our ignorance about the number of species on the planet
Before going on to look at how humans are causing the extinction of species, it might help to give some idea of how many species there are on the planet today. Despite all the advances in the various disciplines in science, to our shame, we humans have no idea how many species share this planet with us. There is no central database on the planet which lists the number of species. We are particularly ignorant of species living in the oceans. A total of 210,000 species of marine animals and plants are known to science. The true number could be close to 2 million. Recently, in an area off New Caledonia in the South Pacific, marine scientists found 130,000 mollusks belonging to 3,000 species in just three cubic metres of coral reef.[3]

The English zoologist Colin Tudge remarks that we know

---

3. Steve Connor, 'Scientists discover 500 species of fish in a billion-dollar trawl of the world's oceans', *The Independent*, 24 October 2003, page 1.

more about the stars than about our companion species on earth.[4] The inventory at Kew Gardens outside London, one of the best in the world, lists about 1.7 million species. But Tudge argues that this falls short of the true figure by a factor of 10 or maybe even 100.[5] He recounts Terry Erwin's research in Panama where he anaesthetised and counted the species of beetles found in a single tree in Panama. The figure ran to almost 20,000 and the unknown species far outnumbered the known ones. On the basis of this data Erwin suggested that there might be 30 million species on the planet – most of them insects. Tudge comments that, while some biologists consider Erwin's figure of 30 million to be a gross exaggeration, others argue that it is too conservative and would prefer to put the figure at around 100 million.

Many of these species are nematodes, mites and microbes. The known inventory of microbes both bacterial and archaeal species stands at around 40,000. But this may only be a small percentage of the total number. Tudge feels that this gross ignorance about our living world should humble us humans into the clear recognition of the fact that our grasp of 'biodiversity' is tenuous indeed. And that only accounts for creatures that are living on the planet with us now. If we include all the creatures that have lived on the planet since life emerged 3.8 billion years ago, the number of living creatures reaches dizzy heights.[6] The tragedy is that we are wiping out a significant percentage of these creatures – small and large – before we even have recognised their presence with us on our shared planet.

Given the *caveat* about our knowledge of the number of species on the planet, it is now estimated that 24% of large animals, 30% of the known 25,000 fish species, 12% of the 10,000 bird species are now in danger of extinction. Other endangered species are well-known and closely related to humankind. *Time* magazine (31 January 2000) estimates that many of our close

4. Colin Tudge, *The Variety of Life, A Survey and Celebration of All the Creatures that have ever LIVED*, Oxford University Press, Oxford, 2000, page 7.
5. Ibid., pages 6 and 7.
6. Ibid., pages 8 and 9.

cousins among primates are on the brink of extinction. These include orangutans, mountain gorillas, golden bamboo lemur and Hainan gibbons. The growing trade in bush meat in Africa is decimating the remaining populations of gorillas, chimpanzees and other primates.[7]

Big game hunters have decimated the rhino population. Today fewer than 12,000 survive in Africa and Asia. The demand for ivory has led to a precipitous decline in the African rhino from 2 million in 1970 to under 500,000 today. Tigers are also facing extinction. In 1996 it was estimated that the wild population was between 4,600 and 7,200. The largest cat in the world, the Siberian tiger, is down to a mere 200 individuals.[8]

While researching this book I was surprised to find that one creature – a species of giant guinea pig called capybara – was facing extinction as a direct result of Catholic faith and practice. This creature is found in Venezuela and is a particular favourite during the period of Lent. During colonial times, the Holy See ruled that this semi-aquatic mammal was a fish and therefore could be eaten during Lent when Catholics were required to abstain from eating meat. The demand for the capybara has been so great in recent times that Dr Edgar Useche, who advises Venezuela's National Assembly, says that the species could now face extinction.[9]

As the extinction of one species has a knock-on effect on at least 16 other species, this projected level of extinction is an extraordinary blow to the global web of life.[10] No wonder an article in *Time* magazine in 2000 concluded with a very pertinent question: 'How long will Earth be a hospitable place for humanity when it is no longer a fit home for our next of kin?'[11]

Human activity is causing extinction in three ways:

7. 'Now, It's Not Personal! But like it or not, meat-eating is becoming a problem for everyone on the planet', editors, *Word-Watch*, July/August 2004, page 19.
8. McGreal, Chris, 'Lions face new threat; the're rich, American and they've got guns', *The Guardian*, 27 April 2001, page 3.
9. NOTEBOOK, 'Fishy Meat', *The Tablet*, 12 April 2003, page 13.
10. Donella Meadows, Jorgen Randers, Dennis Meadows, op.cit., page 85.
11. Charles, P. Alexander, 'Death Row', *Time*, 31 Jan 2000, pages 62-65.

- Habitat destruction.
- The introduction of alien, exotic species into an ecosystem.
- And, finally, human-created pollution.

In the following pages I will look briefly at how each one of these factors is impoverishing our planet.

Habitat Destruction

Let us take habitat destruction first. I very quickly became aware of the massive destruction of species in South Cotabato in the Philippines. The Philippines is one of only 17 countries on earth that are rich in biodiversity. More than 52,177 species have been described. Half of these are found nowhere else on earth. According to the *Philippine Biodiversity Conservation Priorities,* 'the Philippines is one of the few countries in the world that is both a megadiversity country and a biodiversity hotspot.'[12] The document goes on to say that there 'is a small window of opportunity in which it is still possible to save this global hotspot from complete devastation and the unique life forms found within from extinction.'[13]

Tropical forests teem with a rich variety of plants, animals, reptiles, birds, insects and fish species. In a single hectare of rainforest one might find over 100 different species of trees, with countless other species as well. With the destruction of rainforests in Asia, Africa, Central and Latin America and New Guinea, tens of thousands of species have already been lost.[14]

How Philippine forests were felled

At the beginning of the 20th century, 70% of the land area of the Philippines enjoyed forest cover. During the Spanish period the main pressure on the forests came from ship building, the spread of commercial agriculture – abaca, tobacco and sugar-

---

12. *Philippine Biodiversity Conservation Priorities: National Biodiversity Strategy and Action Plan, Executive Summary,* Department of the Environment and Natural Resources, Quezon Avenue, 1101 Quezon City, Philippines, 2002.
13. Ibid.
14. Janet N. Abramovitz, April 1998, 'Taking a Stand: Cultivating a New Relationship with the World's Forests', *WorldWatch Paper 140,* page 5.

cane and cattle ranches. The new US administration took over from the Spanish after a bloody war in 1898 in which almost 200,000 Filipinos were killed. The US colonial administration sought ways to stimulate the Philippine economy. One very lucrative way was to promote commercial logging for export. There was huge demand for Philippine hardwood in the US, Europe and Australia and US logging companies were ready to move in to cut the trees. It was presented as a win-win situation. By 1920, forest cover had shrunk to 60%. Logging increased during the 1930s. Much commercial logging was suspended during World War II but it started immediately after the war. By 1950 forest cover had shrunk to 50%.

The real logging boom took place in the 1960s and 1970s. There was a frenetic effort to clear as much forest as possible in a short period of time. By the 1970s, forest cover was down to 34%. The high point in forest destruction took place between 1977 and 1980. An estimated 300,000 hectares were destroyed each year. Many of the central islands – Cebu, Bohol, Siquirjor, Samar and Camiguin – had been completely denuded. By 1987 only 23% forest cover remained.[15] In 1999 forest cover was estimated at 5.5 million hectares or 18.3% of the land area. Unfortunately, of this only 800,000 hectares are of primary forest cover. This constitutes only 2.7% of the total land area.[16]

Though the profits from logging were astronomical, they benefited only a few elite families. It is estimated that between 1960 and the late 1970s a mere 480 timber licensees enjoyed a staggering profit of US $42 billion.[17] Given the enormous amount of money involved, it is easy to understand how much corruption surrounded the forestry business. One statistic illustrates this. Between 1980 and 1982 the Japanese inventories of log imports from the Philippines were 250% above the official Philippines figures.[18] Securing a logging permit guaranteed a person millions of dollars. Logging benefited US and European

15. *Decline of the Philippine Forests*, op. cit., page 16.
16. Ibid., page 22.
17. Ibid., page 18.
18. Ibid., page 16.

transnational logging companies, the Philippine elite, some military officers and other politicians, most of whom were allied to the dictator, Ferdinand Marcos. Japanese companies became involved with Filipino business people in joint ventures in the 1970s and Koreans followed suit in the 1980s.

Hardly a dollar of this huge amount of money was spent improving the lives of tribal people, like the T'boli, right across the Philippines through provision of schools, clinics, agricultural programmes or other livelihood initiatives. Their habitat, which had supported their tribe for over 1,000 years, was plundered and laid to waste.

Another negative consequence of logging was the construction of logging roads into places that, until then, were impregnable to outsiders. The logging roads became arteries for lowland Christian Filipinos from both the island of Luzon and the Visayas to enter into the tribal lands. Within a generation these settlers came to own the best land in the tribal areas through both legal and illegal transactions. The loss of ancestral lands, through a variety of mechanisms, explains why the armed conflict between some Muslims groups and the Philippine government has continued for the past few decades.

Laying waste the forest destroys biodiversity. The Philippine forests were particularly rich in fauna, estimated at about 2 million species many of which are indigenous to the Philippines.[19] This breakdown includes over 20,000 species of plants and 13,000 species of flowering plants. There are 3,000 species of trees, mostly of the diphtercocarpaceae family. In addition there are untold species of mosses, fungi, epiphytes, algae and 556 species of birds. It is known that 43 species of birds are now threatened with extinction, including the world famous Philippine eagle. The destruction of the rainforest in the Philippines has taken a huge toll on these magnificent birds. Even though pockets or small areas of the forest survive, these 'islands of forests' are not sufficient to guarantee the survival of the Philippine eagle which requires large areas of woodland in

19. Ibid., pages 21-22.

order to live and propagate. Today fewer than 500 birds remain in the wild. With its habitat destroyed, this magnificent bird faces extinction. While living in the mountains of South Cotabato in Mindanao I saw one of the last remaining Philippine eagles. It was a magnificent creature, over three feet tall and a wing span of over five feet. But my delight at seeing it was tinged with sadness, knowing that I was a member of the last generation of human beings that would have the privilege of seeing such splendid birds in the wild. Finally, of the estimated 153 mammal species in the Philippines, 32 are facing extinction.[20]

In addition, the plants, berries, nuts, fish and other creatures found in the rainforest are used as food by the tribal people who live there. The biogeographer Chris Park estimates that there are 75,000 edible plants in the world. Many of these plants found around the globe, especially in rainforests, are highly nutritious and could be added to the larder of a much greater proportion of humankind. At the moment, the vast majority of humans are dependent on only 200 plants and animals for their food. In fact cereals like rice, maize, wheat and rye, and root crops like potatoes, form the staple diet for half of the world's population. On the meat side of the food chain, a mere 10 species of birds and wild animals provide the genetic material on which 98% of all livestock product is based globally.[21] With rapid extinction, many species may be gone before their food value is discovered. Even for selfish human reasons it is important that the habitat of these plants be protected so that humans can use them for food in the future.

Species from the rainforest are also important in maintaining and improving human health worldwide. Medicines for many diseases are derived from rainforest flora and fauna. For the past three centuries quinine, derived from the Indian name *quinaquina*, has been used to treat malaria. In recent years the

20. John Tuxill, 'Losing Strands in the Web of Life', *WorldWatch*, May 1998, page 41.
21. Belden C. Lane, 'Biodiversity and the Holy Trinity', *America*, 17 December 2001, pages 7-11.

survival rate of children with lymphatic leukaemia has been greatly enhanced by a drug derived from the rose periwinkle. This plant was originally found in the rainforest of Madagascar. Madagascar, because of its geography, is particularly rich in species. In the eastern forests there are 12,000 recorded species of plants and 190,000 known animal species. 60% of the above are found nowhere else on earth. 90% of that forest is now gone.[22]

In his *Requiem for the Philippine Forests,* Juna Terra lists a number of Philippine medicinal plants found in the forests. *Talung-punay (Datura Alba)* is used for asthma attacks, *duhat (Eugenia jam-bolana)* is used for diabetes, *sambong (Bluema balsamifera)* for high blood pressure and dudua seeds help cure tuberculosis.[23] The possibilities of finding cures for many common illnesses in the flora and fauna of the tropical rainforests are endless.

Because of their long evolutionary journey, there are millions of plants that could conceivably be used as antibiotics, anti-cancer drugs or painkillers. In June 2001, British scientists reported that they had dramatic success in developing the anti-cancer drug combretastatin which is made from the bark of an African tree.[24] Less than 1% of the 250,000 tropical plants have been screened for their pharmaceutical potential.[25]

It would be sheer lunacy if this rich treasure chest was lost to future generations. A case in point is a frog species found in the Australian rainforest that swallowed her own eggs, incubated them in her stomach and gave birth through her mouth. On examination it was found that this species of frog had the ability to switch off her stomach acids while carrying her young. Discovering how this extraordinary feat was achieved would no doubt help pharmaceutical companies develop effective treat-

22. Donella Meadows, Jorgen Randers, Dennis Meadows, op. cit., page 85.
23. June Terra, 'A requiem for the Philippine forests', unpublished, 1989, *Nature*, Kensington Gardens Square, London, W2 4BG.
24. Meek, James, 'Cancer drug made from bark', *The Guardian*, 15 June 2001.
25. Tim Radford, 'Species struggle as humans grab resources', *The Guardian*, 2 August 2002, page 7.

ments for people who suffer from stomach complaints. The knowledge which was written in the genes of this creature may never be known as it became extinct in 1980.

It is estimated that over 50% of 150 prescribed drugs, with an economic value of over $80 billion dollars, are derived from discoveries in the wild. Professor Edward Wilson is convinced that 'it is no exaggeration to say that the search for natural medicine is a race between science and extinction, and will become critically so as more forests fall and coral reefs bleach out and disintegrate.'[26]

The destruction of the forest has increased soil erosion. Soil from denuded hillsides is carried down to the sea during monsoon rains or typhoons. The sediment affects everything – rivers, irrigation canals and coral reefs.

The future of the Philippine forests looks very bleak. Large scale logging is no longer going on because, except for the island of Palawan, most of the trees are gone. If there is no concerted effort to protect what is left and to promote reforestation with native species, forest cover will be down to 6% by the year 2010. This will have a massive impact on sustainable agriculture, not alone on the uplands and the people living there, but on all the islands. Upland areas constitute over 56% of the land area of the country. These uplands have slopes of 18 degrees or more. There needs to be more than 40% forest cover in tropical islands like the Philippines in order to facilitate sustainable agriculture, especially in the lowland farms that depend on irrigation. When the trees are cut, flash floods speed down the hills destroying everything in their path. Little water has been stored by trees, other vegetation and the soil, so rivers and irrigation canals dry up during the dry season. The Philippines without the rainforest will be an impoverished environment with more and more soil erosion with each monsoon and typhoon period.

Now that the Philippine forests have been plundered, the logging companies have moved elsewhere. At the moment they are devastating Indonesia, the Amazon, Siberia, Myanmar

---

26. Edward O. Wilson, op. cit., page 123.

(Burma) and New Guinea. It cannot continue indefinitely, because we live in a finite planet.

Water Ecosystems

Extinction is not confined to plants and trees. Many species of fish and marine life are also threatened. There are three reasons why fish and other species are disappearing from our oceans. Over-fishing, the destruction of sensitive habitats like coral reefs and mangrove forests, and chemical pollutants are destroying many marine creatures. In 2002 the Food and Agriculture Organisation of the United Nations estimated that 75% of the world's oceanic fisheries were stretched beyond their capacity. In 9 of the 19 world fishing zones, fish catches were above the lower limit of estimated sustainable yield.[27]

According to logbooks in fishing trawlers, some species like the hammerhead have dropped by 89% since 1886. The stocks of blue fin tuna have dropped by 80% in the western Atlantic since the 1960s. Cod, which was once so common in our fish and chip shops, is on the endangered species list. The stocks in both the North Sea and Irish Sea have been decimated. Atlantic halibut has almost disappeared.

Seahorses are also heavily exploited both for aquariums and Chinese medicine. This is a very lucrative trade. Top quality dried seahorses have sold for up to $1,200 per kilogram in Hong Kong. In the late 1990s over 20 million animals were being caught each year. The demand in China has grown during the past few years. The stocks globally cannot sustain such pressure. 36 species of seahorses are under threat at the moment.[28]

There has been a 50% drop in shark numbers in the past 15 years. Blue shark numbers have also dropped by 60%.

One of the programmes in the BBC's Blue Planet series was called 'Deep Trouble'. The programme was narrated by Martha

27. Donella Meadows, Jorgen Randers, Dennis Meadows, op. cit., page 231.
28. John Tuxill, 'Losing Strands in the Web of Life', *EarthWatch Papers*, May 1998, page 37.

Holmes, a marine biologist and member of the David Attenborough team. She concentrated on the damage that humans were doing both to the oceans and to marine ecosystems like coral reefs and mangrove forests.

The programme estimated that about 100 million sharks are being caught each year. These wonderful creatures are being slaughtered, mainly for their fins. Shark fins are worth hundreds of dollars in some Asian countries.[29] They are both a delicacy and a resource for traditional medicine.

The threat to the oceans and creatures living in the oceans is not confined to those living close to the surface. Fishermen can now trawl the bottom of the ocean and catch fish that could not be seen until 20 years ago. They do this in the most destructive way by pulling huge nets along the bottom of the sea and in the process they destroy corals and sponges and everything that has grown on the sea floor for hundreds of years. One New Zealand marine biologist, who was interviewed on the programme, compared modern fishing methods for deep water fish to a farmer who wished to catch a cow by suspending a net from a helicopter and trawling it across his fields. Besides catching the cow he would also capture the car, the dog, a few sheep and his wife. Everything would then be discarded except the cow. That is what happens in much of modern fishing techniques.

Coral Reefs

A number of marine environments are under threat. Coral reefs are the tropical forests of the oceans. There are almost 1,000 coral species found right around the world. Many have developed over hundreds of years and are spectacular in size and architecture. They range from cabbage to moose antlers and mushroom corals. They are replete with an extraordinary array of marine life. Coral reefs account for 25% of the total fish catch in many Third World countries. In Asia alone corals provide sea food for about one billion people. The wonderful structure of the corals provides animals and fish with a safe habitat in which to

29. Tim Radford, 'It scared you stiff, now the great white faces its own', *The Guardian*, 17 January 2003, page 3.

breed and to feed. They also protect mangroves and sea grass beds which also act as nurseries for fish and shellfish. Philippine coral fauna is one of the richest in the world, with over 430 species. Recently, for example, a new species of coral belonging to the genus *leptoseris* was discovered in the Kalayaan Islands.[30]

During my 20 years in the Philippines in the 1970s and 1980s I spent many hours snorkelling around reefs. I came to love the magic of coral reefs, their magnificent shapes and the pastel colours of the reef fish as they dash in and out of the coral cover. Corals are truly a wonderland which leave Disneyland, with all its gadgetry, in the shade. It is estimated that 60% of reef-associated fish are found in the Philippines. Once again it is a place of extraordinary riches in biodiversity.[31]

Luxury fish like groupers and humphead rass are being sought in coral reefs around the globe. Regrettably they are being fished out at an unsustainable level. Martha Holmes discovered that 30,000 tonnes of reef fish pass through Hong Kong each year. As stocks in reefs in nearby countries are depleted, fishing boats have to seek out new coral reefs, often 3,000 miles away. Marine biologists are worried that much of the catch is now composed of juveniles. One does not need to be a marine biologist to realise that when the bulk of the global catch are juveniles, the end is in sight for that species. Harvesting fish at a critical point in the life cycle before they can reproduce jeopardises the future of the species. It is killing the goose that lays the golden egg!

A 1997 study on coral reefs co-ordinated by the University of Hong Kong found that coral reefs around the world are in a lamentable state. Researchers checked 300 reefs in 30 countries and found that a mere 32% of the reefs had living corals. This means that 68% were barren or seriously degraded. The Caribbean had the lowest rate of living corals at 22%. South East Asia was just a little better off with 30% living cover. Marine scientist Edgardo Gomez of the University of the Philippines estimates that 90% of

---

30. *Philippine Biodiversity Conservation Priorities*, op. cit., page 51.
31. Ibid., page 52.

the Philippines' 34,000 sq km of reefs are dead or deteriorating.[32]

I witnessed the widespread disappearance of corals through siltation from deforestation and monocrop industrial agriculture during the 1970s and 1980s. Corals live in symbiotic relationship with zooxanthellae that depend on sunlight for photosynthesis. The silt washed down from the hills and mountains as a result of deforestation interferes with photosynthesis and as a result the corals die.

Walking along beaches in the province of Misamis Occidental I often heard a loud clap as dynamite was used to stun and kill fish. In some ways it is an efficient way of catching fish today. But it ensures that there will be no fish tomorrow, and a single blast can wipe out a patch of coral and destroy something that has been building up for decades. Dynamiting can also take its toll on the fishermen. The fisherman needs to be very dextrous in lighting the fuse and timing to the moment when he throws the bottle with the dynamite into the water. If he throws too soon the wick will quench. There is very little margin for error and unfortunately many lose a hand as the bottle with the dynamite blows up in their hands. On the beaches of Misamis Occidental I met many men who had lost one hand and a few who had lost both. I was very aware that many of these people took what appears to us as a foolhardy decision, because they were living in dire poverty and needed food immediately.

Cyanide is also used to stun fish, especially for the aquarium trade to First World countries. When cyanide is squirted into crevices in the reef the fish that rush out in search of oxygen are easily caught. The fish do not die immediately but their internal organs begin to collapse. By this time unscrupulous merchants have sold off the aquarium fish to buyers in Europe, Japan or the US. Within a few weeks the fish die but the aquarium owner may feel that their death was due to natural causes or was caused by faults in their fish tank. The corals themselves also die

32. J. Madeleine Nash, 'Assault of the Reefs', *Time*, 28 October 1996, The supplement on the State of the Planet, Oceans.

after being sprayed with the poison. Within a few weeks a fertile and beautiful ecosystem disintegrates and is covered with algae.

Cold water corrals are far more numerous than previously thought. These are found in many parts of the world at depths between 3,000 and 12,000 feet, including on the continental shelf off the coast of Ireland. These are being destroyed by bottom-dredging trawlers that use heavy chains, steel plates and nets. Klaus Toepfer, the executive director of the United Nations Environment Programme (UNEP), has called for international agreements to protect these fragile, and little understood, ecosystems from destruction.[33]

Mangrove Forests

Mangrove forests are another ecosystem in the shallow oceans that are under threat. There are 54 mangrove species in the world comprising 16 families. 35 of these species are found in the Philippines.[34] Like the coral reefs they are an extraordinarily productive life system and provide food and shelter for breeding fish. The intricate root system provides a nursery for young fish and protects them from larger predators. When the fish mature they can move out to the reefs and open ocean. Mangroves also collect sediment from the land run-offs. This stabilises the sediment inflow and allows coral to thrive in an area where there might be too much silt for corals to grow and thrive. Mangroves also protect coastlines in many tropical countries from the ravages of storms and typhoons.

Unfortunately, mangrove forests often get a bad press. All that is often seen is the twisted root systems of the trees, and insects, especially mosquitoes that carry disease. They also emit unpleasant odours so that many people, especially those in urban areas, are delighted to see them destroyed and replaced by fish ponds, houses or hotels. There is also the erroneous belief that mangroves and wetlands were essentially wastelands and that they should be substituted by more productive endeavours

33. Steve Connor, 'Cold-water coral put at risk by deep-sea fishing', *The Independent*, 5 June 2004, page 17.
34. *Philippine Biodiversity Conservation Priorities*, op. cit., page 49.

like shrimp farms. In fact mangroves are much more productive and more sustainable than these commercial ventures. On a visit to the island of Negros in the Western Visayas in April 2004, I saw mile after mile of mangrove forests which in the 1980s had been destroyed to make way for shrimp farms. 20 years later they are now abandoned because of the intrusion of salt water into the aquifers. So instead of having a thriving ecosystem which could provide fish for the local population, much of the coastline is now effectively dead. The destruction of mangroves is a tragedy.

At the beginning of the 20th century it was estimated that there were between 400,000 and 500,000 hectares of mangrove forests in the Philippines.[35] By 1994 the figure was down to 120,000 hectares. The expansion of fish farming in these tropical countries has contributed to the destruction of mangroves in recent times. Much the same kind of destruction has happened in other Asian countries. During the past 30 years, millions of hectares of mangrove forests have been destroyed. Thailand lost 27% of its mangroves, Malaysia 20%, Indonesia 40%.

Loss of Bird Species

There are almost 10,000 species of birds on earth. They pollinate crops, control insects and rodents, sow seeds and their beauty and freedom have provided inspiration for humans in all societies since the beginning of humankind.

It is estimated that there are 576 species of birds in the Philippines of which 395 are resident breeders. Of the resident species 195 species are endemic and a further 126 are restricted range species.[36] The Philippines supports a significant number of endangered species for a country of its size. Unfortunately many of these are threatened with extinction as their habitat is lost through logging, shifting agriculture and a growing human population looking for space.[37]

During the past two centuries, 103 species have become ex-

---

35. Ibid., page 49.
36. Ibid., page 45.
37. Ibid., page 45.

tinct, including the once numerous North American passenger
pigeon. A survey published by BirdLife International in the year
2000 estimates that 1,186 species could become extinct in this
century and a further 6,000 could face major decline.[38] The reason why birds are threatened is primarily because of habitat
loss. In Europe over half of all birds depend on agricultural land
for their winter or summer habitat. The change from diverse
farming practices to monocropping large prairie-like fields has
taken a huge toll on bird populations.[39] 9.4 million hectares of
forest cover is lost each year and this includes plantations which
serve bird populations very poorly. As with plant life, the greatest damage is taking place where tropical forests are being destroyed. Migrant birds are threatened when wetlands are
drained for housing or agriculture. Other factors causing the decline include hunting, the use of chemicals and other forms of
pollution.

Oil spills at sea, like the *Exxon Valdez* in 1989 and *Prestige* in
December 2002, wreak havoc on bird life. It is estimated that the
Exxon Valdez disaster killed over 250,000 birds. A 1999 spill off
the coast of France killed between 100,000 and 200,000 birds of
40 different species. The January 2001 oil spill off the famous
Galapagos Islands threatened many endemic species including
the lava gull which is one of the rarest gulls in the world.

The destruction of wetlands in Ireland is having a negative
impact on bird species. According to a document prepared for
BirdWatch Ireland, significant numbers of the world population
of many species come to Irish wetlands in winter. This includes
50% of the Greenland White-fronted Goose population. As of
2002 there were 56 wetland sites which qualify for international
recognition for one or more species of wetland birds.[40] Within
Ireland, 7 of the 18 Red-listed species rely on wetland habitats

---

38. Howard Youth, 'The Plight of Birds', *WorldWatch*, May/June 2002,
page 20.
39. John Tuxill, 'The Biodiversity that People Made', *WorldWatch*, May/
June 2002, page 27.
40. BirdWatch Ireland Policy on the Water Framework Directive and
Nature Conservation: December 2002, Policy No. 02-02, page 3.

for some part of their life-cycle. These include black-necked Grebe, Common Scoter, Corncrake, Lapwing, Curlew, Red-necked Phalarope and the Hen Harrier.[41]

Cats and foxes have also taken their toll on birds, especially ground-nesters. Hunters do enormous damage to bird life in places like Malta, Greece, Italy and France. Television and mobile phone masts also cause damage. 121,000 birds of 123 different species were killed by a 960 foot television tower in Eau Claire, Wisconsin between 1957 and 1994.[42]

Impact of Exotic Species

The introduction of alien or exotic species can have a destructive impact on the native flora and fauna. The reason for this is that in their new habitat there may not be any predator which will control their population levels and limit their spread.

Australia

One of the classic examples of the disastrous consequences of introducing alien species was the introduction of European rabbits into Australia by a Thomas Austin in 1859. Mr Austin was feeling homesick for the animals of his native England (though rabbits were only introduced to England with the Normans after the Battle of Hastings in 1066). Only two dozen rabbits were initially introduced into Mr Austin's farm in Victoria. Because there were no predators – foxes or weasels – they spread rapidly. At the end of 6 years 20,000 had been shot. But 10,000 remained and these spread rapidly across much of the continent devouring everything in their path – grass, shrubs and even trees. Within 50 years they had become such a major problem for farmers and the Australian agricultural economy that the government constructed the famous 2000 miles long 'Rabbit Fence' in an attempt to stop rabbits from moving into the grain areas of South Western Australia. Eventually a few rabbits breached the Rabbit Fence and began the process of multiplying rapidly again.

---

41. Ibid., page 3.
42. Ibid., page 27.

Rabbits are not the only exotic species causing devastation to ecosystems in Australia. The Central American cane toad was introduced to Northern Queensland in 1935 in an attempt to control the grubs of the cane beetle, which were infesting the sugar cane crop. The cane toad did not clear up the beetle problem but it has been devastating everything else in its path. The toads are huge, weighing 4 pounds, and feed on native animals from frogs to bees. They are also poisonous so no predator will eat them. They have moved right through Queensland and are now threatening the Kakadu national park, one of the few unspoilt wildernesses left in the world. This park is home to 340 species of birds and mammals, 55 kinds of freshwater fish, 1,000 kinds of plants.[43] If many of these species are affected it could be a terrible blow for biodiversity.

New Zealand

Australia in turn has been an exporter of exotic pests. In 1837 the bush-tailed opossums were released in New Zealand with the intention of beginning a fur industry. By the 1930s the marsupial had been released in 450 locations and the population levels were completely out of control. They now number over 70 million and are destroying plants, trees and many native bird species. Controlling them is costing the New Zealand taxpayer huge amounts of money.

Hawaii

Today many consider that Hawaii is a beautiful and idyllic place, the ideal location for a vacation close to nature. It comes as a shock to learn that many of the plant, animal and insect species, including the leis that one receives as a welcoming gesture at the airport, are not native to Hawaii. The truth is that the original flora and fauna have been decimated by the arrival of humans. Before the Polynesians arrived somewhere around AD 1400, it was a unique and diverse habitat. It supported somewhere between 124 and 145 species of birds. Many of these were

---

43. David Ficking, 'Australia's plague ready to leap again', *The Guardian*, 22 November 2002, page 22.

flightless birds that foraged on the ground. Today only 35 species of the endemic birds survive and 24 of those species are endangered. The early Polynesians hunted many of the flightless birds to extinction. Many of the birds that visitors see – like skylarks, hill robins, bush warblers, mynahs, rice and red-crested cardinals – are not native to the islands. They arrived in Hawaii in the past 600 years. Among the exotic species brought in by white settlers in the 19th century was the large West African snail. These snails now threaten the much smaller local snail population.

The same story holds for the plant life. 902 of the reported 1,935 species of flowering plants are alien. Before humans arrived there were over 10,000 varieties of plants and animals in Hawaii. Only a fraction remains. The biologist Edward O. Wilson mourns the loss when he writes: 'Ancient Hawaii is a ghost that haunts the hills, and our planet is the poorer for its sad retreat.'[44] One reason for the scale of the destruction is that the native organisms were generally small and therefore vulnerable. The introduction of pigs and rats and big-headed ants had an enormous impact on native species. The latter – big headed ants – known as *Pheidole magacephala*, were responsible for the extinction of many native insect species including those that pollinate native flowering species. There are now over 100,000 feral pigs in the wild and they wreak havoc on trees and other plants.

United States

In Florida, Texas and Louisiana a water hyacinth, originally from South America, is clogging many waterways and costing a fortune to control. Purple loosestrife, introduced into the US in the 19th century, has now spread to almost every part of the US and Canada, especially in freshwater marshes. Unfortunately it competes with native species for food and also eliminates them.

What were known as 'Acclimatization Societies' were formed in many cities in Australia, New Zealand and the US in order to introduce European species into their locality. While

44. Edward O. Wilson, *The Future of Life*, Little Brown, London, 2001, pages 44-45.

they may have reminded immigrants of their homeland, many of the introduced species did damage to the local environment. One did not need to introduce a whole flock to begin the cycle of damage. European starlings began with the release of a single pair in New York. Now they form vast colonies. They are considered a pest by many farmers because they eat their grain and fruit. In the aviation world they are considered a hazard for planes that are taking off or landing.

Among insects the 'killer bee' had reached the US by 1990. This Africanised honeybee is quite aggressive. At least 5 people are known to have died from its sting since 1990. This is a case of an experiment gone wrong, as the bees accidentally escaped from a hybridisation project in Brazil in the mid-1950s. Swarms have spread over South America in the past 40 years.

Africa

In East Africa the introduction of Nile perch into Lake Victoria in the early 1950s has had a devastating impact on the native cichlids. This, like the Galapagos Island, is one of the privileged places on the planet for understanding evolutionary biology and species differentiation. This lake is the second largest freshwater lake in the world. It supported 300 specialised species of cichlids. The Nile perch preyed on the smaller cichlids and destroyed their food sources. It is estimated that 60 percent of the Lake Victoria cichlids may now be extinct.[45] By 1985 almost 90% of fish caught in the Lake were Nile Perch.

Ireland

It will be interesting to see what the impact of zebra mussels will be on Irish lakes and rivers. This mussel was introduced into Ireland in the 1990s and has now spread far and wide, especially in the Shannon river system. It is extremely prolific in freshwater lakes and rivers and is clogging up water intake pipes for reservoirs and utility companies. The zebra mussel was introduced to the Great Lakes in the US, probably in ballast water, in the mid-1980s. It is now present in all the Great Lakes as well as other

---

45. John Tulill, op. cit., pages 36-37.

rivers and lakes in the Eastern US. The US Fisheries and Wildlife Service estimate that the cost of destruction by the zebra mussel to the US economy would be $5 billion by the year 2002.[46]

Also in Ireland, the introduction of New Zealand flatworms in potted plants is becoming a menace in many parts of the country. On the flora front, the introduction of rhododendron to Ireland two centuries ago has had a negative impact on native flora. The rhododendrons colonise infertile, acid soil, elbowing out native species. It blocks out light for other creatures and, according to Dr Declan Little, 'it has no enemies and its tough, leathery leaves are unpalatable to virtually all invertebrates'.[47]

As I know very well from observing our woods at Dalgan Park, Navan, the introduction of the grey squirrel has done enormous damage to the young trees. The squirrels eat the young shoots and strip the bark of young trees which kills or deforms the trees. The dispersal of grey squirrels has been rampant since they were introduced into Ireland in 1911. They have also effectively banished the red squirrels which were resident in Dalgan when I was student there in the 1960s. The red squirrels are much smaller and lighter.

Another unwelcome visitor is the Varroa mite which was introduced into Ireland in the 1990s. It is having a devastating impact on the bee industry and the knock-on effect on agriculture and horticulture could be enormous. The mites infest bees and live on their blood. As a result the bees are weakened and have a much shorter life span. In severe infestations the bees can be deformed, with stunted wings and shortened abdomens. It is estimated that a colony of bees will die 3 or 4 years after infestation. Bees with the mite were imported into Sligo in the early 1990s. Over the past decade, varroa has spread rapidly and is in the process of infesting much of the feral bee population and also domestic hives right across the country. The negative consequence for fruit of the destruction of bees is huge. While bee-

---

46. Edward O. Wilson, *The Future of Life*, op. cit., page 72.
47. Dr Declan Little, 'Native Irish Woodlands', *WildIreland*, May/June 2003, page 30.

keeping associations are alarmed at the spread of varroa, the
response of the Irish government to date has been minimal.

In our globalised world where goods and people move
around the world with such ease, one can expect an increase in
exotic species in the years to come. Freight containers can now
deliver exotic species well beyond the port of entry of any country – right into its heartland. Many believe that the Asian Tiger
mosquito was introduced into US, Australia and New Zealand
in containers carrying used tyres. Air travel also provides an
ideal environment for the transport of mosquitoes and other insects. The outbreak of foot-and-mouth in Britain in 2002 was fac-
ilitated by infected offal which came from outside the country.
In an ever more globalised world, especially if sanitary inspect-
ors are not available at every port or airport, one can expect
more exotic species will find their way to different parts of the
world.

Human-created Pollution
Oil exploration and chemical and heavy metal pollutants from
industry in the lower Volga have virtually destroyed the
Caspian Sea, the largest inland body of water in the world, cov-
ering an area of 4,000 square miles. Drilling for oil began in 1874.
By the early 1880s one hundred refineries were located in the
area. The oil boom generated wealth for a few people. The oil
business continued under the communist regime. With the collapse of the USSR in the late 1980s, western oil corporations
began to invest in the area again. Environmentalists claim that
some of the coast of Azerbaijan is severely polluted with phe-
nols and oil products. For decades much of the heavy industry
of the former USSR was located on the Volga. The river flushed
heavy metals, chemical waste and untreated sewage into the
sea. As a result, miscarriages, stillbirths and congenital deformi-
ties are very common. The coastline of Kazakhstan is equally
polluted. Diseases like tuberculosis and blood diseases are four
times higher near the coast than elsewhere in the country. Many
of the drinking water wells are polluted with oil spills.

Other species are faring no better. Fisheries have almost col-

lapsed. In 1985, 30,000 tons of fish were taken, while the annual catch in the late 1990s was down to 2,100 tons. The Azerbaijan Centre for the Protection of Birds claims that thousands of birds have died from oil contamination. Unless remedial action is taken very soon, the Caspian will follow the Aral Sea as a testimony to human greed and destruction.

Oil spills elsewhere are taking their toll on species around the world. In January 2001 the Ecuadorian tanker *Jessica* ran aground in the bay of San Cristobal and spilled 150,000 gallons of diesel near the Galapagos archipelago. This is one of the most fragile and untouched ecosystems in the world. Though the islands are probably best known for their giant tortoises, they contain 28 unique species of birds, including the lava gull. This is the rarest gull in the world. Birds, especially sea birds, are particularly vulnerable to oil slicks. Even if the birds are not ensnared by the oil slick, there are other long-term dangers. When the oil sinks to the bottom it can destroy marine life, especially algae. This, in turn, endangers the food chain on which fish, birds and other species are dependent.[48]

The pollution at the Galapagos Islands is particularly significant. These islands have a hallowed place in the history of biology because of Charles Darwin's visit in 1835. Darwin's observation about the variation of the islands' bird population helped him, at a later date, to formulate a theory of evolution.

Chemicals used in agriculture and disease control, like DDT, have also had a devastating impact on bird life. DDT built up in the fatty tissue of fish-eating birds and almost caused a collapse among peregrines, eagles and ospreys. After DDT was banned in many First World countries in the early 1970s, these species recovered. The production, use and disposal of Polyvinyl Chloride (PVC) creates toxic pollution. Much of it ends up in water systems and eventually in the oceans.

---

48. Alex Bellos and John Vidal, 'Galapagos oil "catastrophe"', *The Guardian*, 23 January 2001.

Amphibians

In the 1980s, scientists and many observers of the natural world began to notice the drastic decline in frog populations right around the world. While there does not seem to be one single explanation for the drastic collapse, a number of factors are at work in both local ecosystems and globally. The mountain yellow-legged frog of the Sierra Madre in California has vanished because of predation by non-native species like trout. In other parts of the world, the frog population has come under threat from exposure to organochlorines in herbicides and pesticides. Heavy metals such as cadmium, zinc, aluminium, copper and iron are toxic to frogs. The depletion of the ozone layer has also taken its toll as excessive ultraviolet rays of the sun damage frogs' eggs.[49] In the State of Minnesota many frogs are exhibiting growth abnormalities. Some are missing limbs, others have extra limbs. The cause seems to be chemical pollution from methoprene which is sprayed on ponds to inhibit the growth of mosquito larvae.[50] Frogs are also under threat because their habitat has shrunk in recent decades.

Global Warming

The most worrying and pervasive form of pollution is human-induced global warming. The atmospheric concentration of carbon dioxide, methane, chloroflourocarbons (CFCs) and other 'greenhouse' gases is expected to increase by 30% during the next 50 years. A study by a group of scientists in preparation for the international meeting on global warming in the Hague in November 2000 suggests that 'the upper range of warming over the next 100 years could be far higher than was estimated in 1995.'[51]

Global warming will cause major, and in the main, deleterious climatic changes. In Northern latitudes winters will probably be shorter and wetter. Sub-tropical areas might become drier

---

49. John Tuxill, op. cit., page 5.
50. Edward O. Wilson, *The Future of Life*, page 55.
51. John Vidal, 'Global warming is greater than predicted – study', *The Irish Times*, 27 October 2000.

and more arid, and tropical ones wetter. The changes will have major, but as yet unpredictable, effects on agriculture and natural eco-systems. Most plants and animals live in places with very limited temperature ranges. Sir David King, the British Government's chief scientific consultant, believes that, with the present warming trends, cities like London, New York and New Orleans will be inundated by rising ocean levels as the Arctic and Antarctic icecaps melt.[52] He could also have included many cities in Third World countries from Cairo to Manila. There is now more carbon dioxide in the atmosphere than at any period for the past 55 million years. Ice cores from the Antarctic show that during the ice ages the level of carbon dioxide in the atmosphere was 200 parts per million (ppm). During warm periods it reached about 270 ppm. In 1990 it had reached 360 ppm and in 2004 it is at 379 ppm. It is increasing at 3 ppm per year. Sir David said that we do not know how much carbon dioxide was in the atmosphere 55 million years ago when all the ice caps on the planet had melted, but it was probably only slightly more than we are 'currently heading towards'.[53]

In the summer of 2004, scientists studying Greenland's ice cover found that it was melting at the rate of ten metres per year, not one metre as previously thought. If the entire Greenland ice sheet melted, they said, this would raise the level of the oceans globally by seven metres; as a result many heavily populated areas of the world, like Bangladesh, would be flooded. Scientists studying Greenland's vast ice sheet admit that there is no way they can give a timetable for ice melting, but they are worried by the data from the current study which suggests a much quicker timetable for the rise of the oceans than previously thought.[54]

In January 2004 Dr Chris Thomas, professor of Conservation Biology at Leeds University, published an article in the magazine *Nature* on the impact of global warming on the natural

52. Paul Brown, 'Melting ice would wipe out London – top scientist', *The Guardian*, 14 July 2004, pages 1-2.
53. Ibid.
54. Hamish MacDonnell, 'Scientists alarmed at ten-fold increase in melt rate of Greenland ice-sheet', *The Scotsman*, 4 August 2004, page 9.

world. He and his team estimate that over the next 50 years climate change is expected to drive one quarter of land animals and
plants into extinction. The paper is based on two years of research involving scientists from all over the world. According to
Professor Thomas, 'when scientists set about research they hope
to come up with definite results, but what we found we wish we
had not. It is far, far worse than we thought, and what we have
discovered may be an underestimate.'[55]

We also know that after the last ice age it took centuries for
the present flora and fauna to become established in a particular
place. Now habitat change is taking place so rapidly, and the
natural world is dissected with roads, farms, villages, towns and
cities which will make it even more difficult for species to adapt
to the new, unpredictable climatic conditions.

Among the most startling findings was that of the 24 species
of butterfly studied in Australia, all but three would disappear
in their current range, and half would become extinct.[56] Global
warming is also affecting mudflats and salt marshes. Migratory
birds, for example, may find that the salt marshes and mudflats
on which they depend for food will disappear even with a relatively small rise in the levels of the ocean.

In June 2004, scientists at the Sir Alistair Hardy Foundation
for Ocean Science in Plymouth warned that warmer conditions
in the North Sea could have a catastrophic effect on the coastal
ecosystems. Hundreds of seemingly healthy birds were found
dead on the Norfolk coastline in the early months of 2004.
Initially scientists blamed a major pollution incident. Now they
seem to think that climate change is eliminating stocks of plankton and other micro-organisms on which all marine life depends. As the foundation of the food chain begins to disappear,
fish and the birds that feed on them, like guillemots and puffins,
are starving to death in areas where they have lived for thousands of years. In the Shetlands, for example, thousands of kitti-

55. Paul Brown, 'An Unnatural disaster', *The Guardian*, 8 January 2004,
page 1.
56. Ibid.

wakes and guillemots, regarded as one of the hardiest of species in the British Isles, have failed to return to their nesting sites. The director of the Foundation, Dr Chris Reid, believes that the temperature and conditions in the North Sea are beginning to resemble the Mediterranean of the east coast of Spain and that the cold water plankton which supported a huge array of species has now moved 1,000 km further north.[57] *Seabird 2000*, a national census of seabirds, recorded 172,000 guillemots in that year. In the summer of 2004 almost no births were recorded, according to Peter Ellis, Shetland area manager for the Royal Society for the Protection of Birds (RSPB). Almost 6,800 pairs of great skuas were recorded in the Shetlands in the same census. This year only a handful of chicks have been hatched. The arctic skuas stood at 1,120 pairs in the census. They failed to produce any young this year.[58]

Global warming is also having an impact on coral reefs. Dr Richard Aronson has compiled a study on the effects of global warming on coral reefs. He says that 'in his own life-time stunning underwater landscapes (reefs) now look like hell.'[59] Already 25% of the world's coral have been wiped out or extensively damaged by warming oceans, pollution and disease. Higher water temperatures have produced a 'bleaching' effect on the corals which kills the corals. The El Niño of 1997-98 boosted by global warming produced the hottest tropical temperatures ever recorded. That event alone destroyed 16% of the world's corals. Many Australians feel that global warming could devastate the Great Barrier Reef within the next 50 years.

Extinction in Ireland
Before the 20th century, some flora and fauna had become ex-

57. Mark Townsend and Richard Sadier, 'North Sea Birds dying as waters heat up', *The Observer*, 20 June 2004. Taken from www. society. guardian.co.uk/environment/story/0,14124,1243929,00html, 6/22/2004, page 1-3.
58. Michael McCarthy, 'Disaster at sea: global warming hits UK birds', *The Independent*, 30 July 2004, page 1.
59. Nicholas Christian, 'Reefs in hot water as climate changes', *Scotland on Sunday*, 15 February 2004, page 22.

tinct in Ireland. The Irish elk is a typical example, as is the Irish wolf. Wolves had roamed Ireland for thousands of years before humans arrived. Their contemporaries in Ireland would have included giant Irish deer, woolly mammoths and bears. They shared the island with humans for thousands of years. For much of that period there were wilderness areas in Ireland and the human population did not exceed 1.5 million.

Wolves were hunted by humans because they preyed on domestic animals and therefore were seen as a nuisance. In 1655 the Cromwellian authorities set generous bounties for wolves. A female was worth £6, a male £5 and a juvenile fetched £3. This was a huge amount of money and obviously led to the killing of many wolves at that time. The decline in the wolf population accelerated in the late 16th and early 17th centuries. The last wolf was killed in Carlow in 1786 by a farmer who was irate that he had lost so many sheep to a lone wolf in Mount Leinster.[60] Dr Kieran Hickey points out that the extinction of the wolf greatly impoverished the very poor indigenous mammalian species in Ireland. 'Only for the introduction of a number of mammals which have gone wild, for example, the rabbit, hedgehog and grey squirrel, Ireland would have one of the poorest mammalian faunas of any area of its size anywhere in the world.'[61]

Since the middle of the 20th century, intensive petrochemical agriculture and building programmes have taken a huge toll on the environment in Ireland. Three species of wild flowers – corn cockle, corn chamomile and shepherd's needle – have become extinct in recent years. When I was growing up in the 1950s, clumps of cowslips, buttercups, blue bells and primroses decorated most fields. They have almost all vanished and have been replaced by ubiquitous monotonous ryegrass.

Agricultural practices, massacring of hedges and thoughtless building programmes have silenced birds in recent years. Since World War II much of Britain's ancient meadows, hedgerows

---

60. Dr Kieran Hickey, 'The Wolf, forgotten Irish hunter', *WildIreland*, May/June 2003, pages 10-13.
61. Ibid., page 11.

and woodlands have been destroyed in an effort to create pairie-like environments much loved by the agri-business industry. In the period between 1948-1989, 109,000 miles of hedgerows were destroyed, creating huge fields, some as large as 500 acres. As land holdings increased, many small farmers were forced out of farming. In 1964 there were still a quarter of a million small family farms. By 1989 this number had dropped by more than a half to 120,000 and more have been sold in the last decade.

The number of birds, like larks, yellowhammers, corn buntings and corncrakes, that brought joy to the hearts of previous generations of Irish people, has also dropped significantly. Wetland drainage schemes destroyed the habitat of wetland breeders like the black-necked grebe, the bittern and the marsh harrier. Of course, as Gordon D'Arcy points out in his wonderful book, *Ireland's Lost Birds*, these are not the first birds to be faced with extinction in Ireland.

We have lost the crane, the bittern, the red kite, and a number of species of eagles, the marsh harrier, the osprey, and the goshawk. Woodpeckers were probably present in the original primal forests in Ireland. They became extinct as the forested area of Ireland dwindled to almost zero.[62] These birds have survived in other countries and, theoretically at least, could make a comeback in Ireland. In fact there is a programme under way to re-introduce the golden eagle into Donegal. There is no possibility of a come-back for the great auk. This bird that was once so common is now extinct, not just in Ireland, but globally.[63]

In a period of 7 years in the 1990s, the number of bird species which are endangered in Ireland grew by 50%, according to a study undertaken by BirdWatch Ireland and the Royal Society for the Protection of Birds in Northern Ireland.[64] Species like the curlew, the yellowhammer, the chough and the cuckoo are also under great threat. Their number has declined by more than

62. Dr Declan Little, op. cit., page 30.
63. Gordon D'Arcy, *Ireland's Lost Birds*, Four Court's Press, Dublin, 1999.
64. Sean MacConnell, '18 bird species now endangered', *The Irish Times*, 22 May 2000.

50% during the past 25 years. The decline in bird species is due to intensive chemical agriculture and the destruction of hedges. Dr Purvis, the co-ordinator of a major 5-year study into the environmental health of the Irish countryside, describes the homogenous landscape of high-yielding ryegrass as a 'dairy prairie'. According to him such an environment stripped of hedges will not attract many birds.[65]

During the past 30 years, thousands of kilometres of hedgerows have been removed. The Wildlife Act of 1976, amended in 1999, was designed to restrict the cutting of hedgerows between April 1 and August 15 in order to protect birds during the nesting and breeding period. Though significant financial and custodial sentences are included in the Act, they have not, to date, curbed the practice of cutting hedgerows during late spring and summer. I have not heard of anyone being prosecuted under the Act so it would appear that the authorities are not very serious about protecting birds. The number of song thrush has halved as intensive farming has eliminated their food source – snails, slugs and hedge berries. As long as the agriculture policies that promote specialisation and maximisation of output are in place, the rural environment will continue to decline and more and more creatures will be forced into extinction.

Fish species are also beginning to appear on the extinction list. A study of the World Wide Fund for Nature found that: 'population levels of the Atlantic salmon in a third of the traditional salmon rivers of north America and Europe are endangered and that the 'king of fish' has disappeared from more than 300 out of 2,000 river systems'.[66] Factors generated by human activity are mainly responsible for the decline of the species. Salmon have a special place in Irish mythology and legends about the Fianna. Peter O'Reilly, a veteran salmon angler and

---

65. Liam Reid, 'Dairy prairies blamed for fewer wildlife species', *The Irish Times*, 7 August 2004, page 3.
66. Vidal, John, 'Stocks of wild Atlantic Salmon at record low', *The Guardian*, 1 June 2001, page 6.

author, states that in Ireland there has been a catastrophic collapse in salmon stocks during the past 60 years and especially during the past 30 years.[67]

In May 2002 a Junior Minister refused to take the advice of his own scientists to reduce the catch taken by the drift-net fishermen by 40% in order to save the north Atlantic salmon.[68]

If we wish to have good salmon rivers we need to address issues like pollution, industrialised farming, acid rain, hormone-disrupting chemicals, forestry and urbanisation. The disappearance of salmon should be a wake-up call about the health of the wider environment. To thrive, salmon need clean and well oxygenated water. Once water quality declines, salmon begin to disappear.

Forest Destruction in Ireland

During my years in the T'boli hills I began to make the connections between what was happening in the Philippines and what happened in Ireland over the centuries. Based on pollen analysis, it seems that Juniper was the first tree to reach Ireland after that last glacial period. Pine and hazel followed soon afterwards. By 8,500 BC oak and elm forests were established in areas where the soil was good.[69] By 7,000 years ago, Ireland was covered in forests with oak, ash, elm, Scots pine and birch trees. The original people to reach the shores of Ireland about 9,000 years ago were hunters and gatherers. They were a few small bands and did little to disturb the forest cover. This changed with the introduction of agriculture by 5,500 years ago. Forests were cleared for tillage and grazing. The arrival of the plough about 2,500 years ago further intensified human pressure on the forest.[70] By the year AD 1,000 the dominant feature of the Irish

67. Peter O'Reilly, 'Save our Salmon', *The Irish Independent*, 17 January 2003, page 10.
68. Jack Power, 'Now, it's our turn to be the lepers of Europe', *The Irish Examiner*, 15 May 2002, page 21.
69. David Hickey, *Native Trees and Forests of Ireland*, Gill and Macmillan, 2002, page 4.
70. Dr Declan Little, op. cit., pages 27-31.

landscape was large tracts of open landscape and pasture. The remaining Irish broadleaf forests were destroyed during the second half of the last millennium. In 1600 over 12% of Ireland was still covered by forests. The 17th and 18th centuries saw a concerted attack on Irish forests. They were cut to build ships and great houses, both here and in England, and to make charcoal for the burgeoning iron industry in England. They were also considered a security risk by the English authorities as forests provided cover and protection for Irish rebels.

By the time of the Act of Union in 1800 only 2% of the country was covered in woodland. The pain caused by the destruction of the forests and the demise of the Gaelic, Catholic culture is captured by a Munster poet in the lament *Cill Cais. Cád a dhéanfamid feasta gan adhmaid, tá deireadh na gcoillte ar lár? Níl trácht ar Chill Cais ná a teaghlach is ní chluinfear a cling go brách* (What will we do without timber, as the destruction of the forest is complete? There is no talk now of Cill Cais or the great family that lived there and the bells will never again be heard.)

Irish timber was used during the Napoleonic Wars to build British warships and guns. It was also used for barrel staves in the brewing and distillery industry.

Since the foundation of the State the forest cover in Ireland has increased, but the bulk of the planting, unfortunately, is made up of non-native conifers like Sitka Spruce rather than broadleaf trees. Most of the planting has been done by Coillte Teoranta, the state-owned commercial forestry company. A 2003 report from the EU Commission found that Irish forestry policy pays little heed to the environment and thus was out of step with other European Countries.[71] The Irish government's National Forestry Plan 1996-2030 aims to have 17% of the country covered by forests by the year 2030. Most of the area will be covered with fast growing non-native species.

Given the history of forest exploitation, Irish people should

71. *Environment Watch Ireland*, 'Stop Coillte Destroying Ireland/ Unnatural Forests', www.home.zon.be/ireland22/coillte.htm2003, page 1-2.

be very sensitive to forest destruction anywhere in the world. Regrettably, it would also seem that we Irish have learned nothing from the forest mining that marred our own country during the second half of the last millennium. We are now the largest *per capita* importers of tropical wood in the European Union. We import two and a half times the European average of tropical hardwoods.[72] Imports grew a staggering 64% during the decade between 1977 and 1987. Most of our tropical wood, especially *iroko*, (commonly called teak) comes from West Africa and, especially, the Ivory Coast where the forests are being logged in an unsustainable way. If the present rate of depletion continues, the forests there will be gone within five years. Now that Coilte have signed up to the certification initiative of the international Forest Stewardship Council (FSC) this might change. This certification guarantees the consumer that the wood which is purchased originated in a forest that is managed in a sustainable way and that those involved in logging and transporting are paid just wages. As we will see later, this system is not perfect but it is much better than the free-for-all approach of the so-called 'free-market'.

Bogs are also under threat in Ireland. Blanket and Raised Bog once covered 1,178,798 hectares of Ireland. However, in the past few centuries and, especially the latter half of the 20th century, turf extraction has taken a huge toll on bogs. More than half the peat sold in garden centres in Britain comes from Irish bogs. It is ironic that a hobby like gardening, which one would associate with something positive, can be doing such damage. As Peter Foss, chief executive of Irish Peatland Conservation says: 'We're destroying one habitat to create another fake one in our garden.'[73] At All Saints, a raised bog near Birr in the midlands, roughly 20% of the bog has been dug out by the British firm Leisuregrow despite the fact that this bog has been designated a

---

72. 'Wrong Tree in the Wrong Place, Telling it like it is', *Summit Ireland Ltd.*, Dublin, 2002, page 54.
73. Severin Garrett, 'British gardeners destroy Irish bogs', *The Sunday Tribune*, 27 July 2003, page 8.

Special Area of Conservation and a National Reserve. This site is almost unique in Europe because it has a large birch woodland at its centre.[74] Once the bogs are cleared all that remains is barren land. It would cost too much to reclaim the land for agriculture or forestry.

It was estimated in 2002 that only 18% of bogs have some conservation value. Even much of this is degraded.[75] Peat-burning power stations are also destroying the bogs. As the bogs shrink under the impact of giant turf extractors, the creatures of the bogs are facing an uncertain future. These include two rare species of butterflies, nine different species of dragonflies and a very rare snail, a relic of the last ice age, known as *saxifragea hirculus*. Also under threat are merlin, otter, red grouse, mosses and lichens. A recent survey of Irish bogs by the Irish Peatland Conservation Council (IPCC) revealed that the destruction of peatlands is much more serious then previously thought.[76] Headage subsidies for sheep did enormous damage to blanket bogs on the hills and mountains in the West and South of Ireland.

Likewise, fens have suffered. They now cover only 20% of their original size. The same fate has befallen Turloughs, which are a unique form of wetlands found in limestone areas. Many of these have been drained. Fens provide breeding and feeding locations for many bird species. Twenty-seven different species of birds have been found on the Pollardstown fen in the Midlands. The strands of saw sedge and reed beds provide an ideal location for birds such as Grebe, Mute Swan, Teal, Mallards, Water Rails, Moorhens, Coot and Reed Bunting. 600 different animal species have been recorded on fens in Ireland. The most common of these are invertebrates like beetles, spiders and other insects. The rare Marsh Fritillary butterfly breeds on fens. Its caterpillars survive exclusively on the Devils Bit Scabius. The whorl

---

74. Ibid.
75. *BirdWatch Ireland Policy*, op. cit., page 5.
76. Denise Hall, 'Sod's Law', *The Guardian*, 14 June 2000, page 4 of the supplement.

snail and the Irish Damselfly, both rare and endangered species in Ireland, are found in fens.[77]

Finally, callows, which are another key wetland habitat, are under threat and disappearing. The Shannon callows, formed from seasonal flooding in the middle Shannon, Little Brosna and Suck, are under threat from drainage projects and flood defence embankments.[78] The Shannon callows is one of the few areas in Ireland where the corncrake breeds. Five calling males were located there in the summer of 2004.

Extinction in Britain

Shocked by the experience of food scarcity during World War II, successive governments in the post-war era devised schemes to boost agricultural production, so that Britain would never be vulnerable. This trend was further intensified after Britain entered the Common Market in 1973. Generous agricultural subsidies which, in the main, benefited large well-off farmers, led to even more intensive agricultural production. On the dairy side, for example, milk yields doubled. On the cereal front, wheat production increased five-fold and barley six-fold. Such massive increases were not wrested from the soil without massive social and ecological costs. Larger holdings and increased mechanisation saw many farmers and their children leaving the land with a concomitant rundown in rural services. The ecological costs were also high. There was a dramatic increase in agricultural pollution, from slurry and silage. Nitrate levels and agricultural chemicals pollute the drinking water of many people.

The stark reality is that modern intensive agriculture has totally transformed the countryside. 95% of Britain's traditional hay meadows have been destroyed. 99% of the lowland heaths have vanished, either ploughed up or planted with conifers.

---

77. *Irish Fens*, ENFO Leaflet, 17 St Andrew Street, Dublin 2. Text prepared by Patrick Crushell, Irish Peatland Conservation Council, 119 Capel Street, Dublin 2.
78. *BirdWatch Ireland Policy*, op. cit., page 5.

This intensive agriculture is akin to soil mining. Over 5 million acres are now threatened through soil erosion.[79]

The impact on wildlife is also heavy. In the year 2000, a survey for the Royal Society for the Protection of Birds (RSPB) and the British Trust for Ornithology found the population of birds like larks, corn buntings and grey partridges had fallen in number by over 50% during the past 25 years. The corncrake is almost completely gone – it is no longer in England or Wales and is confined to the western Scottish Isles. I heard it myself on the island of Iona in the mid 1990s. Changes in agricultural methods and the widespread use of pesticides and insecticides reduce the amount of food available for many farmland species of birds. This has lead to the decline in the cuckoo, skylark, corn bunting, yellowhammer, barn owl, curlew and even the thrush. In August 2000 the British government promised to take appropriate steps to stabilise the population of many farmland bird species. What is needed now is definite action programmes.[80]

Trees and plants have also suffered. A United Nations Report in 1992 found that over half the trees in Britain were sick or dying. Only 6% of the country's trees were found to be in good condition compared with 41% in 1989. The report blamed pollution, especially acid rain, for the destruction, though the government preferred to believe the change is due to natural causes.[81] Nineteen species of wildflowers vanished during the 20th century and another 50 are on the endangered list.

The butterfly population is also under threat right across Britain. A report published by Butterfly Conservation, The Centre for Ecology and Hydrology and the Joint Nature Conservation Committee in April 2001 found that of the 59 butterfly species found in Britain, 15 species have declined by more than 50% and five species have become extinct. Once again the

79. Geoffrey Lean, 'Green and Ruined Land', *The Observer Magazine*, 4 June 1989.
80. Rebecca Allison, 'Threat of extinction stalks farmland bird species', *The Guardian*, 20 November 2000, page 12.
81. Geoffrey Lean, 'Half of Britain's trees are sick or dying, says UN report', *The Observer*, 27 September 1992, page 3.

main cause of this collapse is the massive change in land usage that has taken place in recent years. Unless radical conservation steps are taken, the delightful sight of a butterfly flitting across a meadow in summer may soon become a thing of the past.[82]

The peat bogs in Britain have been mined in recent years mainly for use by gardeners. During April 2001 a giant US-owned Scottish company spent £2 million advertising their peat-based compost. The environmental organisation, Friends of the Earth, are opposed to the extraction and selling of peat. They maintain that such practices are destroying the last remnant of the raised bogs in Britain. If the destruction of the bogs continues, rare plants like the great sundew and rare birds like the short-eared owl will face extinction.

The EU's environment commissioner, Margot Wallstrom, wrote in *The Guardian* that in Europe 33 of the vertebrate species are at risk of extinction. They include the Iberian lynx, the European mink and all sea mammals – dolphins, seals and whales.[83]

Extinction spasms in the past

The present 'extinction spasm' is the sixth mass-extinction event in the past 500 million years of life on earth. Scientists now believe that the first mass extinction, which claimed 60% of marine invertebrates, took place at the end of the Ordovician period 440 million years ago. The next occurred at the latter end of the Devonian period, approximately 365 million years ago. Over 90% of the life-forms on the planet were lost in what is known as the boundary of the Permian-Triassic period, about 248 million years ago. There is still a lot of disagreement among scientists about what really happened. Professor Michael J. Benson, in a book entitled *When Life Nearly Died, The Greatest Mass Extinction of All Times*,[84] says that the extinction was sparked by a chain of

---

82. 'Butterflies across Britain threatened by shrinking habitats', *The Guardian*, 25 April 2001, page 13.

83. Margot Wallstrom, 'Disproving Darwin' *The Guardian* (Supplement), 21 January 2004, pages 12 and 13.

84. Professor Michael J. Benson, *When Life Nearly Died, The Greatest Mass Extinction of aAll Times*, Thames and Hudson, London, 2003.

massive volcanic explosions in eastern Russia in what is called the Siberian Traps. The volcanoes also spewed out sulphur dioxide, carbon dioxide and chlorine. This initially led to a drop in temperature as the sun's heat was blocked. The cold snap took its toll on plant life. This was followed by rapid global warming which released huge amounts of methane hydrate into the atmosphere. As the world warmed, the super-concentrated frozen gas methane, which is found on the edges of the polar oceans, was released. This furthered the runaway global warming trend. The warming, in tandem with acid rain, killed many plants. Animals that depended on plants succumbed to starvation. It now appears that there was only a 6 degree increase in global temperature at the time. The Intergovernmental Panel on Climate Change (IPCC) estimates that, unless we change radically, there could be a 6% increase in global temperature by the year 2100. The question arises, could such an increase, which might once again free methane hydrate, have the same impact as it had a quarter of a billion years ago?[85]

Another mass extinction event happened at the end of the Triassic period, 210 million years ago. Once again marine invertebrates were the main casualties. The fifth mass extinction, the best known among non-scientists, happened at the end of the Cretaceous period, 65 million years ago. Scientists believe that it was caused by a meteor which crashed into the Yucatan area of Mexico. It wiped out about 50% of life forms and ended the reign of the dinosaurs.

The present extinction spasm began about 60 years ago with the increased industrialisation of the planet, and a model of economic growth, which demands huge amounts of energy and other resources, was being spread across the globe. It is worth remembering, however, that whenever *homo sapiens* first moved into a new habitat, be it in Australia 60,000 years ago, or in Europe 30,000 years ago, or in the Americas 13,000 years ago, significant numbers of the mega-fauna were pushed over the

---

85. George Monbiot, 'Shadow of Extinction', *The Guardian*, 1 July 2003, page 19.

precipice of extinction within a short period of their arrival. Africa, where *homo sapiens* co-evolved with other creatures, seems to be the only continent where *homo sapiens* lived for a significant period of time without wiping out the mega-fauna.

The current extinction spasm has not been set off by a meteor or other external causes but by the activity of one species. It is now estimated that human activity is causing the extinction of between 70 and 150 species of plants, animals and insects each day.[86] According to the British biologist, Norman Myers, this is one of the greatest setbacks to life's abundance and diversity since the first flickerings of life emerged almost four billion years ago. It is human activity which is destroying the habitat of other creatures, often introducing alien species which have taken such a toll on native species in places like Hawaii. Humans now capture more than 40% of the world's plants and marine growth. This leaves all other species – and estimates run from 7 million to 30 million – to compete for the rest.

Extinction on such a massive scale is so horrendous that it is difficult to grasp. A repeated theme in this book is that many species are being pushed beyond the precipice of extinction before scientists have been able to identify them and decide whether they might be useful as a food or health source for human beings now or in the future.

Destruction of languages and cultures
Before going on to discuss some of the theological dimensions of extinction, it is worthwhile pointing out that the current massive extinction of species is mirrored in the destruction of human cultures and languages. The same economic and political pressures operating at a global level are wiping out cultures, languages and habitats. As a missionary anthropologist, I worked in South Cotabato in Mindanao for 20 years. In that province alone there were six different ethno-linguistic groups. The destruction of the forest and invasion of lowland Filipinos has taken a toll on forests and, therefore, biodiversity, and also on the languages

86. Dick Ahlstrom, 'The slow slide to extinction', *The Irish Times*, 5 April 2003, page 9.

and cultures. Many of them may not survive the 21st century. If they do not, their language, worldview and culture will be lost to humanity. This will be a global impoverishment and an irreversible tragedy.

Some linguists believe that somewhere in the region of 5,000 languages or distinctive dialects became extinct during the 20th century. In North and South America alone, over 1000 languages have disappeared in the past 30 years. The rate at which languages are being lost has been accelerated by social and cultural changes, the introduction of schooling in many hitherto inaccessible places, and the preference which national governments have given to national and international languages.[87]

At the beginning of the third millennium, it is estimated that there are about 6,784 different languages spoken around the globe. According to linguists half of these will become extinct in the next 100 years. The linguist David Crystal puts it very bluntly. '50% means 3,000 languages. To meet this time frame at least one language must die every two weeks or so.'[88] The destruction of cultures and languages is a great loss to humankind.

So too is the global spread of western culture. For example, the ubiquitous spread of fast-food restaurants is undermining local agricultural and food traditions. It also has an adverse impact on the health of those who have abandoned local foods in favour of western fast-foods. In the 1970s I watched while traditional agricultural skills were abandoned in favour of so-called modern, scientific agriculture, even though the traditional methods were far superior in terms of sustainability and soil conservation.

* * *

Extinction of species and the loss of languages and cultural diversity are a great tragedy for the human race and the planet. To date little is being done about this destruction. The reason for

---

87. Hugh Broidy, 'Silent Witnesses', *The Guardian* (Supplement), 28 July 1999, pages 4 and 5.
88. David Crystal, *Language Death*, Cambridge University Press, 2000, page 19.

this is that the small number of people who make crucial economic and political decisions today, whether they are the political leaders of the G8 or the bureaucrats at World Bank, IMF or World Trade Organisation, or the CEOs of mega-corporations, do not appreciate the extent to which the insatiable demands of our global economy are thoroughly tearing apart the web of life, with disastrous consequences for future generations.

I generally refrain from putting a monetary value on nature because, in many ways, it is the supremacy of economic values that has led to so much destruction in nature. Margaret Wallstrom, the EU Environment Commissioner, wrote that experts estimate that nature supplies humans with services worth 26 trillion euro each year.[89] This is seen as 'free' by those who calibrate economic growth, so few people pay any attention to it.

---

89. Margot Wallstrom, op. cit., page 12.

CHAPTER 3

An Adequate Creation Theology

God said, 'Let the earth produce vegetation: seed-bearing plants, and fruit trees bearing fruit with their seeds inside, on earth. And so it was. The earth produced vegetation: plants bearing seed in their several kinds, and trees bearing fruit with their seeds inside in their several kinds. God saw that it was good.'
— Genesis 1:11-13

Why have western people, whose cultures were shaped by the Judeo-Christian and Graeco-Roman heritage, been so neglectful about the rest of creation, especially in recent centuries and decades? Some authors might argue that the central problem in this area stems from Greek culture with its strong distinction between matter and spirit. This was the position taken by René Dubos, the renowned French ecologist and microbiologist, in *Wooing the Earth* – that there was extensive environmental degradation long before the rise of the biblical tradition.[1] Dubos wrote his book in response to an important lecture which the American historian, Lynn White, delivered in 1966. In this lecture White indicted the Christian tradition and maintained that the present ecological problems would continue until there is a major shift in westerners' religious consciousness.[2]

While one may not agree completely with White, we Christians need to acknowledge that, despite orthodox teaching on creation, the incarnation and the sacraments, we have had an ambivalent relationship with the natural world and even our own bodies. Almost from the very beginning, a dualism between matter and spirit, already present in European consciousness

1. Rene Dubos, *Wooing the Earth*, Charles Scribners' Sons, New York, 1972.
2. Lynn White, 'Historical Roots of our Ecological Crisis', *Science*, 1967, pages 1203-7.

through the influence of Greek philosophy, developed in Christian theology. In many ways it emerged from a misunderstanding of the 'flesh' (*sarx*) and 'spirit' (*pneuma*) in the New Testament and especially in the Pauline writings. For Paul *sarx* was not the body or material element but everything in our human make-up that is or can be opposed to the life of the Spirit. *Pneuma*, on the other hand is everything in our human nature that promotes the life of the Spirit. Walter Principe points out that when Paul speaks of the pride of some false teachers in Colossians 2:18, he writes that they were 'puffed up by their minds of flesh' (*nous tes sarkos*).[3]

The Fathers of the Church
The Fathers of the Church, beginning with the early Apologists like Justin Martyr and Theophilus of Antioch, developed a theology of creation. The creation theology of some authors, like Hippolytus of Rome in the second century, was very Christo-centric. 'This wood of the Cross is mine for my eternal salvation ... This tree, which stretches up to the sky, goes from earth to heaven. Immortal plant, stands midway between heaven and earth, a strong prop for the universe, binding all things together ...'[4]

Many of the Fathers elaborated their theology of creation in opposition to the prevailing teachings of Gnosticism and Manichaeism. The Gnostics believed that salvation was reserved for a select minority of the elect who had access to secret knowledge. They also tended to despise the material world and basic bodily functions like eating and, especially, sexuality.

Manichaeism, on the other hand, emerged from the writings of a second century native of Persia called Mani (c. 216-276). He believed in absolute dualism between good and evil, light and darkness. Mani depicted the material world as radically deficient and insisted that the body was evil. The task for the believer

3. Walter Principe, 'Aquinas' Spirituality for Christ's Faithful Living in the World', *The Thomist*, Summer 1992, pages 110-31.
4. Quoted in Cardinal Cahal B. Daly's, *The Minding of Planet Earth*, Veritas, Dublin, 2004, page 217. From Henri de Lubac, *Catholicism*, English translation by Lancelot Sheppard, Burns Oates, London, 1950, page 282.

was to liberate the spirit which emanates from a good creator from the body that comes from an evil creator. This could only be achieved by prayer and asceticism.

Though other Fathers affirmed the goodness of creation and the human body, their teaching was sometimes tinged with some of the current thinking of the time. They incorporated elements of Stoicism into their teaching which often saw feelings and human emotions as an obstacle to living the good life, which should be based on one's reason.

Irenaeus of Lyons was born in Asia Minor and worked as a missionary in Lyons around AD 177. He was a disciple of St Polycarp who also came as a missionary to France from the East. Polycarp had been a disciple of St John the Evangelist. So Irenaeus's doctrine goes right back to the beginning of Christianity. He was adamant that creation is not sinful by nature, but rather it is distorted by sin. He attacked the dualism of the Gnostics in his work *Adversus Haereses*. In this work, which was written in Greek, he taught that the God who created the world is the same God who redeemed the world. So everything in the world comes under the sway of the creator. In Book 11, chapter 2 he affirms that the world was not formed by angels or any other kind of being that might have been acting in a way contrary to God's will. No, the world was made by the Father through the Word.[5]

St Augustine (AD 354-430) who was a bishop in Hippo, North Africa and wrote in Latin, has had a major influence on the articulation of Christian theology down through the ages. He developed his theology of creation in his commentaries on the book of Genesis, *De Genesi Ad Litteram, De Genesi ad litteram imperfectus liber* and *De Genesi Contra Manichos*. Everything in the universe was created by God *ex nihilo*. Against some of the prevailing philosophies of the time, he wrote that creation was not mediated by a demiurge. A demiurge was conceived of as an in-

---

5. *Adversus Haereses*, Book 11, Chapter 2, translated by the Rev Alexander Roberts and James Donaldson. Taken from Volume 1 of *The Anti-Nicean Fathers*, American edition, 1885.

termediary entity, partly divine and partly created. God could use such creatures to create matter and thereby not be tainted by any contact with matter which was always viewed as corruptible. Augustine rejected this philosophy. For him everything was created by the Trinitarian God. While there is a basic optimism in his view of creation, in his elaboration of the doctrine of original sin he paints the body and bodily functions in unflattering light. Augustine taught that original sin, with all its negative consequences, is passed on through sexual intercourse. Even though he abandoned Manichaeism, the 8 to 10 years that he spent with this group did affect his perception of the world. According to him, while marriage is good in itself, sexual intercourse involves at least some element of sin.

Augustine also believed that the natural world was so damaged by original sin that it was worth very little unless redeemed by grace, and that redemption was almost always seen to take people out of this world into another better world. Christ is the mediator. He unites in himself both the humanity that had turned away from God through Adam's sin (even though Christ himself was sinless) and also the Godhead on which humanity is totally dependent. Christ through his passion, death and resurrection leads the baptised to our true home which is in heaven.[6] James Good believes that the negative anti-body and anti-sex attitude, which is deeply rooted in the Christian psyche right up to the time of the Second Vatican Council, owes much to the teaching of St Augustine.[7]

Some commentators believe that Augustine misrepresented the views of an early Celtic theologian call Pelagius. Philip Newell writes that 'every theology student has been told about the dangerous heresy of Pelagius, and the derogatory term 'pelagianism' has come to mean any doctrine that gives central place not to the redemptive grace of God but to our own capacity

6. Gerald Bonnar, 'The Incarnation, the Church and the World According to Augustine', *Doctrine and Life*, July / August 2003, page 347.
7. James Good, 'A Theology of the Body: the Legacy of Augustine', *Doctrine and Life*, July / August 2003, page 358.

to save ourselves.'[8] Like many other seemingly black and white
theological controversies, the historical reality is much more
nuanced and complex. Pelagius arrived in Rome in the early
380s and lived as a lay monk. He became a soul friend, or *anam-
chara* in the later Gaelic tradition, to many well-known men and
women in Rome.

Though he wrote on many subjects, almost all his own writing were lost so his teaching comes to us though the jaundiced
eyes of his detractors like Augustine. One of the dominant features in his theological writing is his belief in the essential goodness of God's creation. In a letter to a friend he wrote:

> Look at the animals roaming the forest: God's spirit dwells
> within them. Look at the birds flying across the sky: God's
> spirit dwells within them. Look at the tiny insects crawling in
> the grass: God's spirit dwells within them. There is no crea-
> ture on earth in whom God is absent ... When God pro-
> nounced that his creation was good, it was not only that his
> hand had fashioned every creature: it was that his breath had
> brought every creature to life. ... The presence of God's spirit
> in all living things is what makes them beautiful: and if we
> look with God's eyes, nothing on the earth is ugly.[9]

Because of the pervasive presence of God in all creation,
Pelagius interpreted that the boundaries of the Great Command-
ment to love God and our neighbour extend beyond the human
community to include all creation. According to him, when our
love is directed towards an animal or even a tree we are partici-
pating in the fullness of God's love.[10] This teaching is much
more in tune with the Wisdom literature of the Bible and also
with the more positive approach to nature within Celtic cultures
– where trees, streams, mountains or other natural phenomena
are 'alive' to the presence of the numinous.[11]

8. Philip Newell, *Listening for the Heartbeat of God*, SPCK, London, 1997,
page 8 and 9, taken from Robert Van de Weyer (ed), *The Letters of
Pelagius*, Arthur James, 1995, letter of Pelagius 71.
9. Ibid., page 11.
10. Ibid., letter of Pelagius 72.
11. John Macquarrie, 'Paths in Spirituality', *Irish Spirituality*, ed.

Pelagius fell foul of the ecclesiastical authorities in Rome for a number of reasons. They were critical of his practice of teaching women to read the scriptures, his passion for justice and his practice of distributing his wealth. At this time, the church had come into a position of power and wealth and had become the official religion of the Roman Empire.

What annoyed church officials most, especially Augustine, was his belief that the image of God was to be seen in the face of a new born baby. For Augustine the world was much darker and, because of original sin, humans lacked the image of God until it was restored in baptism. Not that Pelagius denied the presence of evil, but for him evil was like an occupying army fundamentally alien to our nature. He believed that our deepest desires, however sullied by sin or shackled by vice, were for God. He taught that in the depths of people's souls and hearts there is this yearning for the presence of God. In line with this positive cosmology and anthropology, the redemption which was achieved by Christ's life, death and resurrection was all about liberating the essential goodness that is in the human person.[12] Rather than setting nature and grace in opposition, Pelagius taught that both the essential goodness of nature and the grace to chose to follow Christ are gifts from God. He is quite clear, however, that if what we hear in the depths of our heart is not in line with the example and teaching of Jesus in the scriptures then we have not properly listened to the scriptures which should be our guiding norm.[13] Pelagius' teaching sets the stage for a very different perspective on the relationship between the church and the world than the one we find in Augustine's hostile polarity between these entities.

Augustine moved against Pelagius by having him condemned at two diocesan councils of African Bishops in 416. When the bishop of Rome did not immediately condemn Pelagius, his detractors turned to the secular imperial authority

Michael Maher, Veritas, Dublin, page 7.
12. Philip Newell, *Listening for the Heartbeat of God*, op. cit., pages 14-15.
13. Ibid., 19, letter of Pelagius 67.

to have him banished from Rome on 30 April 418. Later in the summer of 418 Pelagius was excommunicated by the Pope. Soon afterwards he returned to Celtic Britain and possibly ended his days in the monastery at Bangor.

Undoubtedly from the early 5th century until relatively re-cently, the western church was impoverished in its understand-ing of the goodness of creation by not taking seriously the teach-ing of Pelagius and opting wholeheartedly instead for Augustine's more pessimistic views. But even in Augustine's more gloomy perspective on the world, where humans are portrayed as living in exile from their true home, there are chinks of light about the goodness of creation. According to Neil Darragh, the proper un-derstanding of this notion of 'exile' 'has a sociological rather than a cosmological importance. That is, it implies a distancing from other people whose values and lifestyles are different from those of the Christian.'[14] In today's world, for example, Christians are challenged to distance themselves from the all-pervasive, materialistic culture which is so dominant worldwide and which is responsible for the exploitation of many people and the destruction of much of creation. This path is unjust and unsus-tainable and is a way of death. Christians are called to reject it so that other human beings and the earth might prosper. In this sense Christians become the salt of the Earth (Mt 5:13). Cardinal Daly reminds us that the 'world' in St John's gospel means alternately the world which rejected Christ and therefore must be rejected by a follower of Christ, but also the world which God loved so much that he sent his only Son to redeem it.[15]

Despite challenging Manichaeism and other body-denying cults, the majority of the Fathers found it difficult to integrate their theology of creation with their understanding of salvation history. Most harboured a dualism which gave precedence to spiritual realities over material ones. This dualistic, hierarchical

14. Neil Darragh, *At Home in the Earth*, Accent Publications, Auckland, New Zealand, 2000, page 35.
15. Cardinal Cahal Daly, *The Minding of Planet* Earth, Veritas, Dublin, 2004, page 115.

perspective continued in classical Christian theology and spirituality for centuries.

Medieval Period – Benedict and Francis

From the seventh century onwards, a network of Benedictine monasteries was established in western Europe. St Benedict of Nursia, the father of western monasticism, decided that the life experience of his monks should revolve around liturgical prayer and manual work. This inclusion of manual work was, in a sense, a revolutionary departure, since Greek and Roman scholars in general showed a disdain for manual work. Manual work was done by slaves, not men of prayer or scholarship. The monks learned to care for the land so that the model of interaction with the natural world to emerge from this tradition might be called the taming of the Earth. It was very much an extension of the garden tradition of the second chapter of Genesis itself. The vow of stability (*stabilitas loci* – stability of place) meant that the monks could not continually move from one place to another after the fertility of the soil had been exhausted. Rather they set about draining the marshes, cutting forests and tilling the soil in a sustainable way. Many of the technologies which the monks introduced into the tradition of European agriculture, far from depleting the soil, actually enhanced its fertility. This care for the earth is captured in the final paragraph of Wendel Berry's book, *The Gift of Good Land*.

> To live we must daily break the body and shed the blood of creation. When we do it knowingly, lovingly, skilfully and reverently it is a sacrament. When we do it ignorantly, greedily, clumsily and destructively it is a desecration. In such a desecration we condemn ourselves to spiritual and moral loneliness and others to want.[16]

Unlike Benedict, St Francis of Assisi (1182-1226) was a nomad at heart. He and his friars, who were street preachers, were constantly on the move. They had no possessions and were

---

16. Wendel Berry, *The Gift of Good Land*, North Point Press, San Francisco, 1981, page 198

expected to live lightly on the Earth, a burden neither to the
Earth nor to those who met their subsistence needs. In opting for
the nomadic life, Francis abandoned any *homo faber* role for the
brothers. There is no urge to remake the world, even in the garden tradition of the Benedictines. The natural world is not seen
from a utilitarian perspective, to provide food, clothing and
shelter for human beings. Rather there is a sense of joy, wonder,
praise and gratitude for the gift of all life. In his 'Canticle of the
Creatures' Francis shows a kinship with, and deep insight into
the heart of all creation – animate and inanimate – which is
probably unique in the whole European experience.[17] The universe and all creatures were created by God, so in Francis' vision
they were truly brothers and sisters.

A Spirituality of Fuga Mundi
Unfortunately the more mainstream medieval spirituality associated with some of the monastic impulses, like *fuga mundi* (flight
from the world), could and did turn into a contempt for the
world (*contemptus mundi*). This spirituality shows a deep ambivalence towards the world and continued in one way or another right up almost to Vatican II. One finds it, for example, in
many liturgical prayers. The collect for Advent: *doceas nos terrena
despicere at amare caelestia* (you teach us to despise the things of
Earth and love the things of heaven) is typical of this earth-deny-
ing spirituality. Love for God was almost always seen in opposition to love for any creature. Furthermore, from the first century
right up to Vatican I in 1870, there has been a deep-seated fear of
pantheism in the Christian tradition. There was a fear that the
beauty of creation could in itself seduce humans and not help
them to appreciate and reverence the author of all creation.
However, what was often condemned as pantheism was the
much more subtle and orthodox idea of panentheism. Those
who espouse this teaching point to God's presence in all things.
But they are not saying that God cannot be found beyond the

---

17. Seán McDonagh, *To Care for the Earth*, Chapman, London, 1986,
pages 131-3.

phenomenal world. They believe that while creation is dependent on God, he does not depend on creation but exists independ-
ently of creation.

The distrust of the world is also to be found in the *Salve
Regina* (Hail Holy Queen) which is recited at the end of the
rosary. I think that one could argue that the rosary did more to
shape the Catholic religious imagination during the second half
of the second millennium than any other popular devotion or
even the liturgy itself. It sees our earthly sojourn as moving
through a valley of tears: *Ad te suspiramus gementes et flentes in
hac lacrimarum valle. Eia ergo advocata nostra, illos tuos misericordes
oculos ad nos converte. Et Jesum benedictum fructum ventris tui,
nobis post hoc exsilium ostende.* (To thee do we send up our sighs
mourning and weeping in this valley of tears. Turn, then, O
most gracious Advocate, thine eyes of mercy upon us, and after
this our exile show unto us the blessed fruit of thy womb, Jesus.)

I am not for a moment saying that the rosary is not a wonderful prayer. I also know that the man who wrote the words and
the music for the *Salve Regina* in the 11th century was called
Herman the lame. He was a paraplegic and every movement
caused him pain. Still it is easy to see how a spirituality shaped
by the *Salve Regina* does not give high priority to protecting the
natural world. If our true home is in heaven and this world is
just a valley of tears, all energies must be devoted to developing
our interior life, saving our souls so that we can make it safely
across the divide to the next world. There is little or no religious
motivation to encourage people to devote themselves to the
earthly task, least of all caring for the earth. In fact the dominant
impetus is to withdraw from the world which is seen as a place
full of temptations and dangers for the interior life.

The Impact of the Black Death

The pessimistic, anti-this-world mood of some of the medieval
period was further strengthened by the trauma of the Black
Death (1347-9) which swept across and ravaged Europe in the
middle of the 14th century. Approximately 25 million people, or
one third of the population of western Europe, perished. For

those who experienced it, the disease seems to have come from nowhere and in many places, like Florence and Venice, it wiped out half the population in a few weeks. Clerical sermons at the time interpreted the plague as a punishment from God. The only protection against it was to embrace a spiritual theology based on prayer, asceticism, mortification and a withdrawal from engagement with the world. So a spirituality developed which was not based on a theology of engagement with the major challenges of the time. This divorce between spiritual theology and systematic theology continued almost right up to Vatican II in the Catholic Church. In 1961, just before Vatican II, Pope John XXIII had to remind Catholics in his encyclical *Mater et Magistra* that: 'the laity must not suppose that they would be acting prudently to lessen their Christian commitment to this passing world. On the contrary, we insist that they must intensify it and increase it continually … Let no one suppose that a life of activity in the world is incompatible with spiritual perfection.[18]

Cardinal Cahal Daly, in his book *The Minding of Planet Earth*, argues that St Francis is not the only Catholic in the second millennium who is sensitive to the wonder and beauty of the natural world. He quotes from St John of the Cross's *Spiritual Canticle*:

O woods and thickets
Planted by the hand of the Beloved,
O Meadow of verdure
Enamelled with flowers,
Say if he has passed you by.

Answer of the Creatures

Scattering a thousand graces
He passed through these groves in haste,
And, looking upon them as he went,
Left them by his glance alone
Clothed with beauty.

---

18. Pope John XXIII, *Mater et Magistra*, 1961, No 254.

Bride

All those that serve
Relate to me a thousand graces of thee
And all wound me the more,
And something they are stammering
Leaves me dying

In his commentary on these stanzas, St John of the Cross says:

To pass through the groves is to create the elements ... Through these, the Bride says, He passed, scattering a thousand graces, because He adorned them with all the creatures, which are full of grace ... And she says, that He passed, because the creatures are, as it were, a trace of the passing of God, whereby are revealed His greatness, power, wisdom and other Divine virtues.[19]

While it is wonderful to be able to point to a number of Catholic theologians and mystics whose deep appreciation of creation touched and shaped their Christian lives, unfortunately they constitute a small minority in a tradition which either disregarded creation or denigrated it.

A negative attitude towards the world received a new lease of life in the Catholic Church with the rise of Jansenism in the 17th century. Bishop Jansen (1585-1638) was a Dutch Catholic theologian who was a professor of theology in Louvain and bishop of Ypres in 1636. He died in 1638 after completing a four volume manuscript called *Augustine*, which was subsequently published in 1640. Jansen taught that the teaching of Augustine on grace, free will and predestination was opposed to what was called the Jesuit school of theology. Jansen amplified Augustine's negative view of nature so his teaching coloured and soured Catholic attitudes to the world for over 200 years.

The Irish theologian James Good believes that Jansenism became a cancer that ate into every corner of European Cathol-

---

19. Taken from Cardinal Daly's *The Minding of the Planet*, Veritas, Dublin, 2004, pages 55 and 56.

icism for the following two centuries.[20] He points out that when
Maynooth began in 1789, six Jansenist professors from the
Sorbonne in Paris were appointed to the new seminary. He
claims that Jansenism had a stranglehold on Maynooth right up
until the 1940s. Throughout the 1920s and 1930s bishops' pastoral
letters were full of warning against the dangers of 'company-keep-
ing' and cross-road dancing. The body, and especially sexuality,
was not to be trusted and little place was given to it in the
Christian life.

One way of experiencing this gulf that developed in the
Catholic tradition between people, their own bodies and the natural world is to contrast its negative sentiments with the words
and mood of Louis Armstrong's song,

What a wonderful World!

I see trees of green, red roses too,
I see them bloom for me and you,
And I think to myself, what a wonderful world.

I see skies of blue, and clouds of white,
The brightness of day and the darkness of night,
And I think to myself, what a wonderful world.

The sentiments of this song are much closer to the gratitude
for creation that one finds in Ps 139:13-14: 'I thank you for the
wonder of myself, for the wonder of your works.'

Distrust and hostility towards the rest of creation almost always go hand in hand with a similar attitude towards the
human body. For centuries, numerous taboos surrounded any
discussion or portrayal of sexuality in many western cultures,
including Ireland. This has changed profoundly in recent
decades. While sexuality was banished to a very private zone in
the past, today it is present in so many spheres of life. Many as-
pects of popular culture, from advertising to the film industry,
are saturated with sexuality. This cheapens and demeans
sexuality, love and human life.

---

20. Good, op.cit., page 359.

The most exploitative portrayal of sexuality in our world today is undoubtedly pornography. In many western countries it is very pervasive. One finds it in magazines in high street newsagents and bookshops and on the Internet. Sally O'Reilly is a psychotherapist who specialises in adolescence and is concerned about the 'relentless and sexually explicit' nature of advertising and other media, which is aimed at young people. Teenagers are constantly being bombarded with sexual imagery through television, advertising, magazines and music videos.

These images are giving young people the message that, in order to be a valuable person, you have to be sexually provocative and attractive. This, in turn, is putting huge pressure on teenagers to conform to this image and to become sexually active at an earlier age.[21]

Pornography, at first glance, might appear to be a liberation from the shackles of previous taboos on sexuality, but in fact it also stems from a profound alienation from the body. In the vast majority of cases, pornography trivialises and exploits the female body rather than the male body. The only response to both of these destructive depictions of the human body is to develop a proper, caring and respectful attitude towards the human body and creation. This will encourage us to celebrate our bodies and our sexuality as gifts from God for ourselves and others. Given the sex scandals in many countries during the past decade, many people might be slow to look to the Catholic Church for inspiration and guidance in developing a more joyful and adequate understanding of sexuality.

This is a pity as there are many resources, both teaching and of personal witness, within the Judeo-Christian tradition that could help us reclaim this vital dimension of human life which has been tarnished and trivialised in the past and today. The theologian Dianne Bergant calls attention to the alluring dimension of the world, the human body, human sexuality and romance which is celebrated so passionately and extravagantly in

---

21. Susan Calnan, 'Does Abstinence ring hollow?', *The Irish Times*, (Health Supplement), 6 July 2004, page 5.

that beautiful poem the Song of Songs. The text does not attempt
to spiritualise the body or the world as many commentators in
former times have attempted to do. 'Rather, human love is an
expression of the natural world and is born because of, and as a
part of, the natural world.'[22]

Stewardship
Stewardship of the earth is an important theme running through
the scriptures. In chapters two and three of the book of Genesis
humans are challenged to be stewards of God's creation and to
live in companionship with the rest of creation. The command of
God to Adam and Eve is 'to till and to keep' (Gen 2:15).

For the People of Israel the demands of stewardship are seen
in the sensitive way they viewed the land. Aware of their origins
as nomads and outcasts, they saw the land as a gift from God.
Among the neighbours of Israel, the land was often seen as the
exclusive property of the king or the ruling class (1 Kings 21).
This was not true in Israel. Land was the heritage of all the people and it was meant to sustain the whole community (Ex 19:5).
But in a deeper way Israel knew that she did not, in fact, own the
land. Yahweh was the true land owner. The cultivators were
only God's tenants; they were stewards and it was clearly recognised that there were certain restrictions on how they might
utilise it:

> The land must not be sold in perpetuity, for the land belongs
> to me and to me you are only strangers and guests (Lev
> 25:23).

The stewardship metaphor has sometimes been criticised as
being excessively human-centred and too simplistic for addressing complex ecological challenges like those outlined in chapters
one and two.[23] Despite these reservations, the ideas and attitudes
involved in stewardship have much to teach this generation that

22. Bergant, Dianne, 'The Greening of the tradition; the wisdom tradition and creation', *Theology Digest*, Summer 2000, page 129.
23. Clare Palmer, 'Stewardship: a case study in environmental ethics' in
Ian Hall, Margaret Goodall, Clare Palmer and John Reader (eds), *The
Earth Beneath, A Critical Guide to Green Theology*, London, SPCK, 1992.

feels there is a technological answer to all environmental challenges. Modern mechanical agriculture, that exploits land to the point of exhaustion in order to maximise short-term profits, has much to re-learn from the wisdom contained in the book of Leviticus.

The disintegration of our creation story

One could say that, with all its problems, a functioning creation story underpinned European culture and religion until the Late Middle Ages. This cosmology was based on the early chapters of the Book of Genesis interpreted through the prism of Greek Philosophy, often with a Platonic tinge. This situated human beings, and all the realities of this world, within a large cosmic canvas. The great chain of Being spanned the whole range of life from what were considered the lowliest creatures right up to the divine mode of being. This vision lacked the evolutionary, emergent perspectives which we associate with modern science. Each species was specially created, immutable, and occupied a fixed position in the overall scheme of things. Nevertheless, creation was seen in a holistic and organic way.

From an organic, spiritual world to a mechanistic, materialistic one

By the beginning of the 17th century, this uneasiness with the adequacy of the traditional story of the cosmos had developed into a divorce between those who still maintained that the Earth was the centre of everything and those, like Copernicus, who argued that the Earth spun on its own axis and also moved around a stationary sun. While this new Copernican theory opened up the immense universe for observation, and gave a more adequate explanation for the movement of heavenly bodies, it came as a profound shock to many people. The dethronement of the Earth from the centre of creation was seen as a challenge both to Ptolemaic astronomy and, more important still, to orthodox theology.

Old stories and cosmologies do not die easily. Ecclesiastical authorities tried to re-establish the old myth with the trial and condemnation of Galileo in 1633, but the damage had already

been done. The trial was deeply resented by the scientific community, not so much at the time, because many of the people in
the philosophical-scientific community in the 17th century also
supported the Ptolemaic theory that the earth was stationary
and that the sun revolved around it. In the 18th and 19th century,
the trial of Galileo, and the fact that he was forced by the Holy
Office to denounce his writings, was often used as an example of
how the Catholic Church was opposed to science. Cardinal Daly
in his book, *The Minding of Planet Earth*, uses the writings of
Annibale Fantoli to revisit the Galileo case and critique and de-
bunk the science-versus-religion myth that the Galileo case is
supposed to illustrate. One of the most damning things for me in
this whole affair was, not so much what happened in the 16th
and 17th centuries, but that as late as the 1960s the Vatican was
still trying cover up its mistakes and discredit Galileo. Monsignor
Pio Paschini, Rector of the Latern University in Rome, was asked
to review the life, work and condemnation of Galileo. He com-
pleted his task in three years and presented it for publication in
1945. 'The Roman authorities, however, judged the book to be
too favourable to Galileo and decided that it was inopportune
that it be published in the original form. The book was eventually
cleared for publication in 1965, when the author, Paschini, was
already two years dead. Even then, alterations were made to the
conclusions arrived at by Paschini himself. No acknowledge-
ment of the changes was made in the text of the work, when it
was published in 1965, with the title *Vita e Opere De Galileo Galilei*
by Pio Paschini.'[24] At this point Vatican II was in its fourth and
final year. Eventually, in 2002, Pope John Paul II expressed profound regret for the weaknesses of so many of (the church's)
sons and daughters in many instances, including the Galileo affair.[25]

However one evaluates the Galileo case, from the late 17th
century onwards science and religion tended to follow separate,
often mutually hostile, paths in the western world. Religious

---

24. Cardinal Cahal Daly, op. cit., page 81.
25. Ibid., page 83.

thinkers withdrew their attentions from wider cosmic, earthly, and even cultural concerns and began to concentrate almost exclusively on the uniqueness of the Christian story. Consequently the theology of creation was generally ignored. Theological enquiry was confined to the process of redemption and salvation, the personality of Jesus, the interior spiritual disciplines needed to guide the individual soul along the path of salvation, and the internal constitution and juridical status of the ecclesial community.

By the mid-sixteenth century, the Reformation had split the western church. Martin Luther (1483-1546), despite his own deep appreciation of nature and the presence of God in nature, followed in the footsteps of St Augustine and taught that all nature had fallen and lay under the judgement of God. The split between the 'spiritual' and 'material' dimension of the universe was actually intensified by Luther's teaching which set the Kingdom of Heaven and the Kingdom of the World in opposition to each other. The Kingdom of Heaven operates under God's grace and love while the Kingdom of the World operates under God's wrath. This same tension exists, for example, between God's rule of power in the world and his rule of grace through the gospel, between the church and the world and between salvation and creation.

The mandate to Adam and Eve in Genesis 1:26-28 is understood in this conflictual framework. While stewardship is seen as important it is not understood as a stewardship of mutual benefit, but is seen within a master-slave relationship. This effectively deprives nature of almost any intrinsic value and, in a secularised context, can allow for its exploitation. Much of the Protestant tradition also tended to reject the traditional natural theology of the scholastics. They insisted on the primacy of salvation and the order of grace and had a more jaundiced, Augustinian view of nature.

It is also important to remember that, during the following centuries, much of the most creative energy in the Christian churches was spent on internecine struggles and rivalry. This left little time for Christian thinkers to understand and interpret the larger cultural and historical movements associated with the Renaissance and the colonial expansion in the Americas, Africa, Asia and Oceania. It also blinded religious thinkers to what was happening in the scientific community in Europe and thus prevented them from understanding the religious significance of the new developments in science.

As discoveries in physics, astronomy, geology and biology followed hard on the heels of each other, the Genesis story began to appear less and less plausible, as did the church itself especially if it was seen to insist on claiming that the first eleven chapters of Genesis were a historical account of the beginnings of creation. For many scientists it appeared little more credible than a fairytale and thus it lost any effective power to guide them in their professional endeavours. Given this religious and cosmological lacuna, it was understandable that many scientists readily adopted the mechanistic, reductionist view of nature in line with the ideas propounded by Isaac Newton and René Descartes. Their reductionist approach viewed nature and even the human body as composed of interchangeable parts that can be repaired and replaced. Above all, nature was composed of dead, inert particles and was moved by external forces rather than forces inherent to creation itself which in contemporary cosmology are marked by creativity, spontaneity and novelty.

In the centuries that followed the Reformation, major scientific figures like Francis Bacon (1561-1626) and René Descartes (1596-1650) put together the building blocks for viewing the world in an exclusively mechanistic way. By the end of the 17th century, John Locke's belief that 'God gave the world to man for him to exploit for his own convenience and benefit' was firmly in place in the prevailing, scientific culture.[26]

It is important to note here that my discussion of the Christian experience and response to the Enlightenment and the scientific revolutions which occurred from the 16th, 17th and

---

26. 'Second Treatise of Government' in P. Laslett ed., *Two Treatises of Government*, Cambridge, CUP, 1963, Chapter V, sections 34-40).

18th centuries is confined more or less to the Catholic tradition for the simple reason that I am a member of that church and I am better acquainted with its traditions.

While much of what I say applies also to the Protestant tradition in Europe and North America, quite a number of Protestants, particularly those of the liberal tradition, entered into a dialogue with the Enlightenment and emerging scientific disciplines of the time, especially in the 19th century. Catholics and many evangelical Protestants saw this as a sell-out and mounted a constant polemic against such tendencies. They pointed out that the liberal Protestant tradition was swamped by the new knowledge and often seduced into abandoning traditional Christian teaching. This resulted in the broad spectrum of Catholic scholarship and much of evangelical Protestantism shying away from any attempt, such as Aquinas had made in his day, to ground the Christian faith on the emerging cosmological insights. Some evangelical churches, especially in the US, still insist on the historicity of the first 11 chapters of Genesis and continue to campaign to have 'creation science' taught in schools

Our Mechanical World

Successive stages of the Industrial Revolution based on steam, petrochemical, electrical and nuclear energy have followed quickly on the heels of each other during the past century. Each phase has delivered into human hands more awesome power to dominate and change the biosphere. Unfortunately, the wisdom which a well-integrated religious view of the cosmos might have generated, was lacking. Such a holistic approach might have directed science and technology to use their power in ways which might enhance all life on earth. Unfortunately it helped despoil nature and cause the present ecological and social crisis.

CHAPTER 4

Theology Forgot Creation

The Earth is at the same time mother,
She is mother of all
For contained in her
Are the seeds of all.
The Earth of humankind
Contains moistness
  all verdancy
  all germinating power.
It is in some many ways fruitful
Yet it forms not only the basic
raw material for humankind
but also the substance of God's Son.
— Hildegard of Bingen.

The topics covered in theology textbooks, throughout the 19th century and right up to Vatican II in the 1960s, illustrate how out of touch religious thinkers were with the fascinating new discoveries in science. Christian theologians focused their attention, almost exclusively, on the reality of the sacred, on the processes of human salvation, on the person of Jesus, the sacraments, the sacred texts, the nature of the church and Canon Law. In this theology, God was seen as the creator of the world, omnipotent but largely removed from the world. While God related to the human community in terms of the theology of redemption, his relation to the rest of creation was minimal. In this worldview, the world was stripped of any mythical or sacral dimension. For all practical purposes, concerns about the natural world, as well as debates about politics, economics and culture, areas of life that were engaging the minds of scholars and thoughtful people, were largely ignored by theologians because they were seen as outside the theological realm.

Recent Catholic Church teaching

Despite the destruction which is taking place in our world, the Christian churches have not responded in any effective way to environmental destruction.

As I argued above, a creation-oriented and sacramental church ought to have been more sensitive to the massive problems that faced the earth in the 20th century. But reflections by prominent Catholic theologians or pronouncements from church leaders were few and far removed, as I outlined in an earlier book, *The Greening of the Church*.[1] Often church officials do not like to hear this and are simply in denial. Archbishop Dermot Clifford is much more honest and truthful when he writes that people like Dag Hammarskjold drew attention to environmental problems in the 1960s long before the church had made any pronouncements.[2]

Rachel Carson's seminal book, *Silent Spring*, was published in April 1962. The Second Vatican Council began in October 1962 and continued until 1966. The Council is undoubtedly the major achievement of the Catholic Church in the 20th century. *Gaudium et Spes* (The Church in the Modern World) is a milestone in the history of the church's stance towards the world. It embodies a positive, liberating vision of life that refuses to seal off religious issues from the rest of human affairs. One cannot, however, argue that it is grounded in an ecological vision of reality. This document subscribes to what is called 'dominion theology': the natural world is there for man's exclusive use, 'for man, created in God's image, received a mandate to subject to himself all that it contains, and govern the world with justice and holiness' (No 34). No 9 of the same document insists that: 'meanwhile the conviction grows that humanity can and should consolidate its control over creation, but even more, that it devolves on humanity to establish a political, social and economic order which will to an even better extent serve man.'

1. Seán McDonagh, *The Greening of the Church*, Chapman, London, 1990, pages 175-203.
2. Archbishop Dermot Clifford, *Lent: The Whole of Creation is Groaning*, Pastoral Letter on the Environment, Lent 2003, page 6.

This anthropocentric bias is even more marked in No 12 of the same document. It claims almost universal agreement for the teaching that: 'according to the unanimous opinion of believers and unbelievers alike, all things on earth should be related to man as their centre and crown'. The cultures of tribal peoples and Hinduism and Buddhism, the great religions of the East, can hardly be used to bolster up this claim.

The Catholic Church was not alone in overlooking creation. The historian Keith Thomas in his book, *Man and the Natural World*, writes that, during the sixteenth century, western literature, theology and popular preaching ascribed no intrinsic value to the natural world. According to the divines and preachers from the Tudor period onwards, humans were unique among all species on the earth. Animals were inert and lacked any spiritual or emotional dimension. Plants and animals were only useful in so far as they met human needs. Gen 1:26-28 was used to promote man's right to subjugate the world.[3]

The first papal document devoted exclusively to environment and development issues, entitled *Peace with God the Creator, Peace with all creation,* was published on 1 January 1990. In it Pope John Paul II draws attention to the moral and religious dimensions of the environmental crisis. He declares that 'Christians in particular realise that their duty towards nature and Creator are an *essential* part of their faith' (No 15, emphasis mine). This teaching is arguably the best kept secret in the Catholic Church.

It is also important to acknowledge that this document is heavily dependent on the Justice, Peace and Integrity of Creation (JPIC) programme, which the World Council of Churches launched at its Assembly in Vancouver in 1983. To its credit, the World Council of Churches is one of the few Christian institutions that has consistently focused its attention on ecology, development, justice and poverty during the past 25 years. It is a pity that the two most recent encyclicals – *Evangelium Vitae* and

3. Keith Thomas, *Man and the Natural World*, Pantheon, New York, 1983, pages 17-30.

Faith and Reason are so engrossed in human problems and moral challenges that they barely mention the current ecological crisis.

The strongest statement from the Pope came in a talk on 17 January 2001. The Pope's tone was more strident as he called for an 'ecological conversion' to avert a global ecological disaster.

However, if one looks at the regions of our planet, one realises immediately that humanity has disappointed the divine expectation. Above all, in our time, man has unhesitatingly devastated wooded plains and valleys, polluted the waters, deformed the earth's habitat, made the air unbreathable, upset the hydrogeological and atmospheric systems, blighted green spaces, implemented uncontrolled forms of industrialisation, humiliating – to use an image of Dante Alighieri ('Paradiso', XXII, 151) – the earth, that flower-bed that is our dwelling.

It is necessary, therefore, to stimulate and sustain the 'ecological conversion' which, over these last decades, has made humanity more sensitive when facing the catastrophe toward which it was moving. Man is no longer 'minister' of the Creator. However, as an autonomous despot, he is beginning to understand that he must finally stop before the abyss.[4]

Given that the Christian churches have arrived at these challenges a little breathless and a little late, they must now make up for lost time and, in co-operation with other faiths, throw all their energies into urgently addressing the challenge of justice, peace and the integrity of creation. Unless this awareness is gained in the very near future, human beings and the rest of the planet's community will be condemned to live amid the ruins of the natural world.

In *Evangelium Vitae*, Pope John Paul II reflects on the threats facing human life in the contemporary world. It is a great pity that such a document concentrated mainly on contraception, abortion and euthanasia. It did not address, in any comprehen-

---

4. Pope John Paul II, 'God made man the steward of creation', *L'Osservatore Romano*, 24 January 2001, page 11.

sive way, the ecological crisis which will profoundly affect tens of millions of people. Tampering with the world's ecological balance appears in a long list of other ills in No 10.

The most important role that the churches can play is to articulate a competent theology of creation. To be credible, good God-talk, or an effective theology of creation, can no longer be based exclusively on an exegesis of religious texts from the Bible or anywhere else. It needs to be grounded in scientific knowledge about the immense and complex journey of the universe during its 15 billion-year story. This begins with the initial flaring forth of the fireball, which is now estimated to have taken place 15 billion years ago. It moves on through the bonding and fabrication of the different elements in the dying moments of the supernova explosions. It tells how, over 5 billion years ago, the solar system with its various planets came into being and evolved. Planet earth was positioned in such a strategic place in relation to the sun that it alone of all the planets could become the only living planet in the solar system. The first glimmer of life stirred in the seas three and a half billion years ago. Later life became more complex and moved inland to colonise and transform a previously barren and desolate planet. In the recent life history, the cenezoic period, there has been an extraordinary fluorescence of life on land, in the seas and in the air, which has culminated in the emergence of humankind with its diverse cultures, traditions and languages.

This magnificent story has been articulated more clearly and comprehensively in its physical manifestation by scientists within their diverse disciplines over the past few decades. At the same time a more interrelated, holistic vision of the world has also emerged. The beauty, fruitfulness and yet fragility of the earth imprinted itself deeply on the consciousness of astronauts who took photographs of the earth from space on their journey to the moon in the late 1960s. These photos of the blue-green planet with a swirl of white cloud against the darkness and lifelessness of the rest of space have helped many people to appreciate the beauty, interconnectedness and vulnerability of life on planet

Earth. These photos have become contemporary icons and are to be found in schools, offices, churches and even on the logos of corporations. Yet there is something lacking in the overall picture of the story as told by members of the scientific community, because it confines itself to the phenomenal world.

It took the genius of Pierre Teilhard de Chardin, a Jesuit mystic and scientist, to tell this story in a way that attempted to bridge the gap between the scientific and religious community. In his books, especially *The Phenomenon of Man* and *The Divine Milieu*, he takes cognisance of the spiritual or numinous dimension of the story of the universe. In telling the story of the emergence of the universe, Teilhard sought to articulate the interdependence of matter and spirit in the overall emergence of the universe, earth, life and conscious life, and thus overcome the dualism which has plagued western thought for the past two millennia. This spiritual dimension of the story is an essential ingredient if men and women are to rebuild dynamic, life-giving relationships with the rest of creation and discard the legacy of alienation from nature fostered by centuries of dualism and mechanistic science.

Teilhard's synthesis sweeps away the traditional dichotomy between the sacred and secular. The human story is seen, not as just the final phase in the evolutionary saga, but as part of the total story of the universe. It is vitally connected to all other realities in the universe, especially other forms of life. Humans are not hermetically sealed off from other creatures. In fact, all creatures of the earth are intimately related physically and biologically and are close cousins. In this perspective, the physical world and other creatures can no longer be viewed either as resources to be manipulated and despoiled according to human whims, or as the unchanging and unimportant backdrop against which human destinies, personal and social, are worked out. They are seen as subjects which should elicit a relationship of communion, rather than objects which are then to be controlled and exploited.

Like any functional, vital story, this new story of the universe must give deeper meaning to our lives and must challenge us to organise our world according to its dictates. It must guide, nourish and encourage us as we abandon the exploitative drive of the past century and a half, and set about building a sustainable, just world. A true appreciation of the story should help us see the madness of eliminating – for all time – the tropical forests and the coral reefs. The wealth of life forms, and the dynamic interplay between them, found in these diverse ecosystems, encodes over one hundred million years of the story of the Earth. It is sheer collective vandalism not to preserve these life-systems for the future.

In short, recourse to this new perspective or paradigm will help us ground all reality on a sure ecological footing instead of the destructive economistic perspective that now values and devalues everything. This is the ultimate context for everything, including human institutions and value systems. This paradigm reminds us that it is foolish to recklessly pursue technological advances without being guided by ecological wisdom, because it threatens the very future of complex life forms on the planet. The story will also guide us as we revisit the scriptures and our spiritual traditions in search of more vital elements in our religious traditions which will help us forge viable global and local theologies of creation.

CHAPTER 5

Theological reflections
in the light of this Mega-Extinction Spasm

The cosmic discipleship of Christ today includes, as an essential element, one's commitment to the practice of ecological concern and care.
— Cho Hyun Chul SJ, *An Ecological Vision of the World*, page 155

In this chapter I will look at the current extinction phase from a religious and theological perspective. I will do this in the light of the new cosmology outlined above, the riches of the biblical tradition, and contemporary Catholic theology.

Fr Thomas Berry, a writer on environmental issues, believes that the destruction of life must be seen as one of the most serious moral issues of our times.

> Extinction is a difficult concept to grasp. It is an eternal concept. It's not at all like the killing of individual life forms that can be renewed through normal processes of reproduction. Nor is it simply diminishing numbers. Nor is it damage that can somehow be remedied or for which some substitute can be found. Nor is it something that simply affects our own generation. Nor is it something that could be remedied by some supernatural power. It is, rather, an absolute and final act for which there is no remedy on earth or in heaven.[1]

The extinction of species is not treated formally in the scriptures. Yet appreciation for life, gratitude to God for the gift of life and a strong belief that God cares for life and wishes humans to emulate this care, are central features of both the Hebrew and Christian scriptures.

In Genesis 1:11-12 the author focuses both on God's act of creating plants and on the self-propagating power with which

---

1. Thomas Berry, *The Dream of the Earth*, Sierra Club Books, San Francisco, 1988, page 9.

he endowed all plant life. We are told that God created seed
bearing plants, and fruit trees with their seeds inside. The verse
ends with the affirmation that 'God saw it was good'. This concern for fruitfulness is also evident in the creation of aquatic life:
'God saw it was good, God blessed them, saying "be fruitful,
multiply and fill the waters of the sea and let the birds multiply
on the earth"'(Gen 1:21-22).

In the second account of creation in chapter 2, creatures exist
because Yahweh breathes his spirit into them. By breathing the
'breath of life' into their nostrils humans become 'living beings'
(Gen 2:7). Humans share the breath of God with other creatures
and all creation as we see in Psalm 33:6: 'By the word of the Lord
the heavens were made, and all their hosts by the breath of his
mouth.' Humans and other creatures only remain alive as long
as God's breath continues to abide with them and sustain them
(Gen 6:3). Much the same point is made in the book of Job when
the author states that without the breath of life everything
would simply cease to exist: 'If he should take back his spirit to
himself, and gather to himself his breath, all flesh would perish
together, all mortals return to dust' (Job 34:14-15). Both of these
are extraordinary statements because they highlight the importance of the immanence of God's presence for all creation.

It is crucial to stress at the outset that the Hebrew scriptures
never discuss life in a philosophical, detached and abstract man-
ner. Rather, life is seen in an active, concrete and, usually, generative way. The Bible is absolutely clear that God is the author of
life. Psalm 139:7-10 celebrates a recurring theme in the Bible,
that God's creative presence accompanies humans no matter
where they go:

Where can I go from your spirit?
Or where can I flee from your presence?
If I should ascend to the heavens you are there,
If I make my bed in Sheol you are there.
If I take the wings of the morning and settle at the farthest
    limits of the sea,
even there your hand shall lead me, your right hand hold
    me fast.

But God is also present in a caring, loving way for all creatures as we see in a text like Psalm 104. He cares for all creation, not merely human beings.

You set springs gushing in ravines,
running down between the mountains,
supplying water for wild animals,
attracting the thirsty wild donkeys,
near there the birds of the air make their nests,
they sing among the leaves (Ps 104:10-12).

God's loving care is summarised in verse 27-28:

All creatures depend on you to feed them throughout the year; you provide the food they eat, with generous hand you satisfy their hunger.

A wonderful passage in the Wisdom of Solomon echoes this common theme that God dwells in, loves in a special way, and enlivens all creatures:

For you love all things that exist,
And detest none of the things you have made,
For you would not have made anything if you had hated it.
How would anything have endured if you had not willed it?
Or how would anything not called forth by you have been
    preserved?
You spare all things, for they are yours, O Lord, you who
    love the living.
For your immortal spirit is in all things (Wisdom 11:24-12:1)

The Bible is aware that many forces work against life in the world. In the Noah story God threatens to chastise humankind because of their sinfulness. 'The earth is full of the violence of man's making, and I will efface them from the earth' (Gen 6:13), and therefore God considers sending a flood which will 'destroy from under heaven all flesh in which is the breath of life' (Gen 6:17).

The story of the flood contains a theme that recurs throughout the Bible, namely, that other creatures also suffer because of human greed and sinfulness. Genesis records that Noah was a good man (Gen 6:8) so God planned to save him and his family from the impending flood waters. God's instructions to Noah included, not merely strategies to save himself and his family, but detailed directions on how to protect other species as well. Noah was told to bring male and female of all creatures, clean, unclean, birds and reptiles, into the safety of the ark, 'so that their lives may be saved' (Gen 6:20). Certainly this care can be seen as a very deliberate act of protecting all the creatures in the community of creation.

It is not surprising then that all the creatures of the earth are party to the covenant which God makes with Noah in the aftermath of the flood. God promises that he will never in the future initiate a catastrophe like the flood. 'See, I establish my Covenant with you and with your descendants after you: also with every living creature to be found with you, birds, cattle and every wild beast with you; everything that came out of the ark, everything that lives on the earth. I establish my Covenant with you: no thing of flesh shall be swept away again by the waters of the flood. There shall be no flood to destroy the earth again' (Gen 9: 9-11).

Respect for Life in the Hebrew Scriptures
The deep respect for all life which runs through the Hebrew scriptures is underscored by the prohibition on eating 'flesh with life, that is blood, in it' (Gen 9:4). For the Hebrews, blood was seen as the seat of life and therefore it was something special and sacred. Humans were not allowed to eat food that contained blood.

The speech by Moses towards the end of the book of Deuteronomy calls on the people of Israel to be faithful to the covenant they made with God on Mount Sinai. He assures them that if they are faithful they will experience blessings; if, on the other hand, they turn away and follow other gods they will be punished. Moses' injunction to 'choose life, so that you and your descendants may live' (Deut 30:19) has a contemporary relevance given the rampant destruction of life through the extinction of species in our contemporary world.

Respect for life can be seen in the institution of the Sabbath which was a day of rest for humans, domestic animals and the land (Ex 23:12 and Deut 5:14-15). The Sabbath benefited both the poor and working animals by ensuring that they were not continuously worked to the point of exhaustion. For the pious Jew the Sabbath was important because it celebrated the fact that even God rested from his work of creation on the seventh day (Gen 2:2-3). Built into the institution of the Sabbath was an ethic of care, moderation and rest (Ex 20:10-11). During the Sabbath year the land was allowed to lie fallow (Lev 25:2-7). The poor and even the wild animals could feast on what they found (Ex 23:11). The intention of the year of Jubilee was that the original order in society and the natural world would be restored, mainly through the forgiveness of debts and the restoration of land to those who had lost it (Lev 25:8-55). It was also a creative way of redistributing wealth in society, something which is still a major challenge in our times where neo-liberal economic policies seem to forget the weak and vulnerable of society.

At the heart of the Sabbath was the belief that life was to be lived and celebrated. It was also clear that one's worth came, not primarily from one's work or possessions, but from knowing that one was loved and blessed by the God of life. The challenge to the pious Jew was to share these good things with others, neighbours, friends and even strangers.

Life is also a recurring theme in the New Testament. The person of Christ is seen as central to all life: 'through him all things came to be' (Jn 1:3). 'He is the bread of life' (Jn 6:48). 'Anyone who eats this bread will live forever; and the bread that I shall give is my flesh, *for the life of the world*' (Jn 6:51). Jesus presents himself as 'the Way, the Truth and the Life' (Jn 14:6). He insists 'I have come that they may have life and have it to the full' (Jn 10:10). Luke 12:24-31 is sometimes quoted to show that Jesus had little appreciation for the natural world. But in fact the text has the opposite meaning. If Yahweh provides for the raven that was understood at the time to be 'unclean', and the common wild flowers, how much more will he care for and provide for the needs of his people?

In the New Testament Jesus, as the Word and Wisdom of God, is active before the dawn of time in the birth of creation out of chaos. Through him the Universe, the Earth, and all life was created (Jn 1:3-4). All the rich unfolding of the universe – from the initial glow of the fireball, through the shaping of the stars and the earth as the green planet of the universe, right up to the emergence of humans and their varied cultures and histories – is centred on Jesus (Col 1:16-17). The incarnation – God assuming a created human form – is an extraordinary affirmation of the goodness and intrinsic value of all creation.

According to the theologian Karl Rahner, the incarnation is the perfect union of the infinite and the finite. Through the incarnation the finite has been given an infinite depth and is no longer a contrast to the infinite, but that which the infinite himself has become in order to open a passage into the infinite for all finite reality. The corporeality assumed by God, which is the human nature of Jesus, has now become the passageway to God for all creatures and all creation. Because of the unity of creation, what took place in Jesus affects and transforms all creation.[2] Christ is the first born of all creation and as such can be seen as an older sibling to all creatures, not merely human beings. Our world, and even the wider universe, is already transformed when viewed from the perspective of the incarnation.

Through his resurrection, Christ is more deeply wedded to the life of the world. In his risen body he is still part of creation but no longer confined to a given cultural and historical period and a particular body. The risen Lord is now present everywhere in creation. The preface for the Mass of Easter Day rejoices in this fact when it states the resurrection 'renews all creation'. The significance of the resurrection of Jesus goes far beyond the remit of the human community and touches all creation.

In reflecting on extinction it is important to remember that every living creature on earth has a profound relationship with

2. Karl Rahner, 'On the Theology of the Incarnation', 115. Quoted in Cho Hyun-Chul SJ, *An Ecological Vision of the World*, Editrice Pontificia Università Gegoriana, Rome, 2004, page 137.

the resurrected Lord. His loving touch heals our brokenness and fulfils all creation. In Acts 3:15 Peter speaks of Jesus as the Prince of Life. Commentators interpret this text as one who leads his people to the fullness of life even if it costs him his own life. Through his death Jesus has reconciled all reality to God. So, to wantonly destroy any aspect of creation, or to banish forever species from their place in the community of life, is to deface the image of Christ which is radiated throughout our world. Christ still suffers, not only when people are denied their rights and exploited, but when seas, rivers, forests are desecrated and biocide is perpetrated. It would be wonderful if the churches could promote a devotion to Christ, the Prince of Life. The royal title is not one of control, or an effort to force others to serve his interests; rather it is the proclamation of God's love and care for those who need it most – the poor and exploited. But today, in the light of environmental destruction, Jesus' preferential option for the poor includes the plundered earth. As the Australian theologian Norman Habel puts it, 'God is found in weakness, in suffering, and in servant earth.'[3]

If one takes seriously the metaphor, the world as the Body of God, developed by the theologian Sally McFague, God's concern for the world is not external or extrinsic. Since God is with all creatures in the depths of being, the suffering of creatures is somehow intrinsically connected with God precisely because the world is the body of God.[4] The scriptures reveal that God is always actively on the side of the poor and the exploited earth. God's presence in this context is experienced as compassion, solidarity and consequent empowerment. This presence often appears to be powerless in the face of injustice or ecological devastation. But it is this powerless presence which, after all, is involved in the cross of Jesus. God's power is revealed in its most extraordinary manifestation in the suffering and death of Christ on the cross. As Cho Hyun-Chul writes, 'it is not divine omni-

---

3. Norman Habel, 'Key Ecojustice Principles' in *Ecotheology*, Sheffield Academic Press Limited, 1998, page 120.
4. Cho Hyun-Chul SJ, op.cit., page 173.

potence but divine vulnerability that will transform the whole
creation into the new creation as was manifested in the resurrection of Jesus, the beginning of the new creation.'[5] God's love,
revealed in the death and resurrection of Jesus, is cosmic and
includes all creatures, and in a special way creatures that are
facing extinction.

The Christian churches, as the midwives of God's reign,
must speak the truth about global environmental destruction in
a much more forthright and unambiguous way. Resurrection
above all brings hope because it guarantees that creation has a
future in God. Based on this foundation, the Christian churches
should be encouraging new ways of living which are much less
destructive than those in place in our throw-away society. The
theological pathways to achieve this reconciliation in the
Christian tradition are through imitating the self-emptying and
unselfishness of Christ. As is clear from Col 1:20, this will often
involve pain and the way of the cross. It will involve standing
with victims, including the suffering Earth and other species,
against the architects of the current destruction.

The Genesis text tells us that human sin destroys our relationship with God, severs human bonds and disfigures creation.
The good news of the gospel is about restoring all these frac-
tured relationships. The 'groaning of creation' that Paul wrote
about in Romans 8:22 is very clear when one examines the current enormous extinction of species. Protecting and restoring
creation must be at the heart of promoting the Reign of God in
our contemporary world. Partiarch Bartholomew of Constant-
inople, spiritual leader of the Orthodox Christians, has said that:

> for humans to cause species to become extinct and to destroy
> the biological diversity of God's creation, for humans to
> degrade the integrity of the earth or its natural forests, or
> destroy its wetlands, for humans to contaminate the earth's
> waters, its land, its air and its life with poisonous substances,
> these are sins.[6]

5. Ibid., page 174.
6. Quoted in Edward O. Wilson, *The Future of Life*, op. cit., page 138.

The Archbishop of Canterbury, Dr Rowan Williams, makes a similar point when he writes that we should be able to see that:

offences against the environment are literally non-sustainable. The argument about ecology has advanced from concerns about 'conservation'. What we now have to confront is that it is also our own 'conservation', our viability as a species that is now at stake.[7]

Denis Edwards points out that in St Bonaventure's theology of the Trinity, God is seen as the source of life and goodness. The focus is not on the essence of God but rather on the dynamic reciprocal relationships that obtain within the Trinity. The Father is seen as the 'Fountain Fullness (fontalis plenitudo) expressing himself in the one who is Image and Word and that this dynamic process reaches its consummation in the one who is the love between them, the Spirit'.[8] This love is not a kind of narcissistic self absorption but a relational and generative love that is the Holy Spirit. The Trinity reveals the full depth and possibility of all relations among humans and in creation while at the same time recognising the importance of individuality. Thus the Trinity becomes an exemplar for enriching the interdependence of ecosystems and deepening the bonds that support human communities and link them to creation. The values which flow from this divine community, and which should be in the forefront of our lives, are mutual love, a willingness to promote life and a commitment to include all creatures in our circle of care. The mutual love of the persons of the Trinity also teaches us that life to the full is only possible in community built on right relationships. Relationships which exclude, alienate or dominate people or the earth lead to death.

Beyond the dynamic love within the Trinity, 'the divine love-life explodes into a thousand forms in the world of creation'. As Belden Lane puts it, 'The Trinity continually seeks out new webs

---

7. Paul Brown, 'Climate change threatens species, says archbishop', *The Guardian*, 6 July 2004, page 9.
8. Denis Edwards, 'Theological Foundations for Ecological Praxis', in *Ecotheology*, Sheffield Academic Press, 1998, page 130.

of interconnectedness, while at the same time remaining separately and wholly itself.'[9] In the light of this Trinitarian interplay, Bonaventure sees creatures as nothing less than a representation of the wisdom of God. Every creature is of its very nature a likeness and resemblance of eternal wisdom and, of course, is brought into existence by the embrace of divine love. Every species, each ecosystem, the earth's biosphere, the universe itself – all are the self expression of divine wisdom.[10] As believers in a God of exuberant love, we are called to celebrate species and genetic diversity not just as a glory of the creation in the cenezoic phase (new life period, 62 million years ago until now) but also as a testimony to the wonder, depth and mystery of God.

In a more recent book on the Creator Spirit, entitled *Breath of Life*, Edwards reminds us that the Spirit of God always accompanies the Word.[11] He feels that in western Christianity, in its theology and spirituality, there has been a tendency to focus exclusively on the Christ person to the exclusion of the Spirit. This, of course, does a great disservice to theology and even christology, as every aspect of the life of Christ from his conception, through his anointing at the Jordan, to his death and resurrection, is touched by the Spirit. Jesus is conceived by the power of the Spirit, sustained by the Spirit in his temptations in the desert and in his ministry, and eventually gifts the church with the Holy Spirit.

Edwards builds his theology of the Spirit against the background of our contemporary cosmology and insights from some of the Eastern Fathers. He finds the work of St Basil of Caesarea particularly helpful. Basil taught that it is the Breath of God (the Spirit) who mediates the divine communion to the world of creatures.[12] The Spirit is seen as the Life-Giver. This aspect of the

---

9. Belden C. Lane, 'Biodiversity and the Holy Trinity', *America*, 17 December 2001, page 10.
10. Ibid., page 130.
11. Denis Edwards, *Breath of Life: A Theology of the Creator Spirit*, Orbis Books, Maryknoll, New York, 2004, page 26.
12. Ibid., page 3.

Spirit is particularly prominent in the writings of St Paul and St John and relevant to our discussion on extinction.

Edwards argues that there is a line of thought in the Fathers of the Eastern tradition which teaches that the involvement of the Spirit is not confined to human redemption and sanctification but also with the creation of the physical world.[13] The Nicean-Constantinopole Creed identifies the Spirit as the giver of life. St Ambrose sees the Spirit as the creator of the whole universe, as the one who brings beauty and grace to creation, and as the one who enables it to exist at every moment. The Spirit is the one who sustains the on-going process of creation.[14] Given our contemporary knowledge of the extraordinary and intricate processes involved in our emergent and evolving universe, it is the Spirit that empowers the whole process to evolve from within in ways that respect the laws of nature that have shaped our universe and the living world. St Basil points out that God's loving care and providence intimately touches every creature. He sees the Creator as the supreme Artist who calls forth a world full of wonderful and diverse creatures that might express and reflect the Wisdom of God.[15] Edwards quotes Michael Schmaus who writes that 'every creature has an indissoluble and indestructible value of its own, simply because it exists, and this individual value is continually created by God'.[16]

Throughout the book, Edwards emphasises both the reciprocity between Word and Spirit and the specific role of each person in relating to creation. He argues: 'If Jesus of Nazareth can be understood as the human face of God in the our midst, the Holy Spirit can be thought of as God present in countless ways that are far beyond the limits of the human. If in Jesus, God is revealed in specific human historical shape, in the Holy Spirit, God is given to us in a personal presence that exceeds the human and transcends human limitations.'[17] Elsewhere he

---

13. Ibid., page 40.
14. Ibid., page 43.
15. Ibid., page 49.
16. Ibid., page 114.
17. Ibid., page 128.

writes that: 'the experience of the presence of the Spirit in the otherness of the nonhuman challenges the kind of anthropocentrism that sees God as focused only on the human. It offers a counter to those who would use religious faith to legitimate the ruthless exploitation of other species. It points to the otherness of nonhuman creatures as a place of God.'[18] It is important that we incorporate this insight into Catholic social teaching which, to date, has little to say about the 'rights' of other creatures to their habitat or place in the biosphere. Even a progressive Catholic development organisation like CIDSE completely overlooks other creatures' needs when it articulates basic Catholic social doctrine. In a position paper on food security, biopatenting and the Trade Related Intellectual Properties (TRIPs) provisions of the World Trade Organisation (WTO), it states that 'the earth and all that is therein is the creation of God and intended for all human beings. The right to private property is just and licit, but all property has a social mortgage.'[19] There is no mention of the rights of other creatures or a biosphere mortgage!

Edwards also sees the Spirit as accompanying all creation in terms of the specificity of each species and the life journey of individuals within the species. The Spirit does this in a way that draws out new possibilities from within the emergent, evolutionary process. The role of the Spirit is not just an impersonal power but rather a personal presence within creatures which enables them to emerge and to evolve, and also works to strengthen their communion with other species in the ecosystem and the whole biosphere.[20] This view of the Spirit as the one who sustains the web of relationships in creation, challenges the traditional dualistic vision of creation with its clear separation of matter and spirit. As we have seen, the dualistic view of creation effectively banishes God from creation and creates a chasm between humankind and the rest of creation. The reality is that

18. Ibid., page 176.
19. CIDSE, May 2001, FAQ on Food Security, Biopatenting and TRIPs, www.cidse.org/pubs, 6/22/2004, page 2.
20. Denis Edwards, *Breath of Life*, page 119.

God is *in* creation, empowering and vivifying it through the power of the Spirit. The Spirit cares for the community of life. Humans are part of the community of life, intimately linked with all creation.

In this vision of creation, community and relationships take precedence over individuality or singularity. Anything that destroys this community or disrupts dynamic and living relationship, like extinction, is anathema to the Spirit of life. In virtue of the dynamic Spirit, all beings in the universe are interrelated and interdependent, forming the community of life.

While creation can be attributed to God, as Persons-in-Communion, Edwards believes that the divine immanent, life-giving presence to the emergent universe is the distinctive role of the Holy Spirit within creation.[21] It is through the Spirit that organisms are maintained in existence and also, over time and given the proper environment, can transcend themselves and become another species through the process of evolution.

The Spirit accompanies each creature with a love that respects each creature's own identity, possibilities and proper autonomy. But the reality of extinction disrupts this 'companioning' by the Spirit. It also forecloses countless possibilities, not just for the species involved, but for other species that depend on that species for their wellbeing and survival within the web of life. It also arrests the evolutionary journey of the biosphere in its tracks, leading to a more sterile planet.

The current extinction saga is also tragic since it is being caused by the humans with whom the Spirit relates in a particular way which is grace-filled, self-conscious (and) dialogical.[22] Edwards is convinced that the Holy Spirit suffers with suffering creation particularly when, as in the case of extinction, irreparable damage is done to the fabric of creation.[23] A sterilised world forecloses future evolutionary possibilities and means that there will be less and less species to delight the companioning Spirit.

---

21. Ibid., page 123.
22. Ibid., page 119.
23. Ibid., page 112.

Contemplating this pain and destruction from the perspective of Christ's death and resurrection, Christians believe that the 'healing, transforming, renewing, refreshing [Spirit] who promises health and wholeness for all creation,' is actively shaping the consciousness of people, both inside and outside the church, who are working at local, national and international level to stop this biocide and protect biodiversity.[24]

Compromising our ability to image God
The present mega-extinction phase is not alone sterilising the planet, undermining its diversity and grieving the Spirit, but it is seriously compromising our ability to develop new insights into the nature of God. As one species after another is jostled over the abyss of extinction, the unique way that each one has of reflecting the divine is lost forever. Saint Bonaventure used the image of the stain-glass window to capture this difference. 'As a ray of light entering through a window is coloured in different ways according to the different colours of the various parts, so the divine ray shines forth in each and every creature in different ways and in different properties.'[25]

St Thomas is also concerned about the sacramental dimension of creation. He makes it clear that the consideration of creatures is useful for the instruction of faith: 'If therefore the goodness, beauty and delightfulness of creatures are so alluring to the minds of men and women, the fountainhead of God's own goodness, compared with the rivulets of goodness found in creatures, will draw the enkindled hearts of all wholly to itself … Consideration [of creatures] endows men with a certain likeness to God's perfection … It is therefore evident that the consideration of creatures has its part to play in building the Christian faith.'[26]

St Thomas goes on to insist on the importance of all the creatures in nature because of the power of each to reveal God in a

24. Ibid., page 171.
25. Denis Edwards, 'Theological Foundations for Ecological Praxis', in *Ecotheology*, Sheffield Academic Press, 1998, page 130.
26. *Summa Contra Gentiles*, ii 2 (translation by James F. Anderson, Image Books, Doubleday, New York, 1956, op. cit., page 48. The quotation is

different way. He argues that God created a magnificent variety of creatures so that his goodness might be communicated to them and reflected by them:

Hence we must say that the distinction and multitude of things comes from the intention of the first agent, who is God. For he brought things into being in order that his goodness might be communicated to creatures and be represented by them; and because his goodness could not be adequately represented by one creature alone, he produced many and diverse creatures so that, what was wanting to one in the manifestation of the divine goodness, might be supplied by another. For goodness, which in God is simple and uniform, in creatures is manifold and divided; and hence the whole universe together participates in the divine goodness more perfectly, and represents it better, than any single creature whatsoever.[27]

St Thomas is saying that no single creature, even humankind, is more important than the whole biosphere. Furthermore, humans came forth in a habitat that was rich in biodiversity. This has shaped not just our biological evolution, but our interior life as well. Our profound and wonderful sense of the divine comes to us to a great extent from the beauty and diversity of the natural world. The Psalmist uses the image of the cedars of Lebanon, while the Book of Exodus compares God's love to that of an eagle who bears her young on her wings (Ex 19:4). So when we extinguish species we destroy the possibilities those species had for representing in a unique way the mystery of God.

Thomas Berry believes that sterilising the planet will also impoverish our imagination. He writes:

'If we have powers of imagination, these are activated by the magic display of colour and sound, of form and movement, such as we observe in the clouds of the sky, the trees and

taken from Cardinal Cahal Daly's, 2004, *The Minding of Planet Earth*, Veritas, Dublin, page 54.)
27. St Thomas Aquinas, *Summa*, Part 1, Question 47, Article 1, *Sancti Thomae Aquinatis*, Biblioteca De Authores Christianos, MCMLVI.

bushes and flowers, the waters and the wind, the singing birds, and the movement of the great blue whale through the sea. If we have words with which to speak and think and commune, words for the inner experience of the divine, words for the intimacies of life, if we can sing, it is again because of the impression we have received from the variety of being around us.

If we lived on the moon, our mind and emotions, our speech, our imagination, our sense of the divine would all reflect the desolation of the lunar landscape.[28]

The poet Patrick Kavanagh put it beautifully when he wrote that nature is 'a window that looks inward to God'.[29] For these reasons I find it difficult to comprehend how the churches, especially those that emphasise a pro-life ethos, have been so silent on extinction. The evil of species extinction does not appear, for example, in the encyclical, *Veritatis Splendor*, which was written by Pope John Paul II to restate Catholic moral teaching in the contemporary world.[30] I am saddened that Catholics, either at the individual or institutional level, have not been 'people of life and for life' to quote the words of Pope John Paul II in *Evangelium Vitae*.[31] It is difficult to comprehend that, in a document named *The Gospel of Life*, the list includes murder, contraception, abortion and suicide but fails to mention the enormity of biocide. This despite the fact that the Pontifical Academy of Sciences reported in 1987 that some 35,000 species were facing extinction by the year 2000. The Pontifical Academy obviously underestimated the calamity but, at least, they raised the issue.[32]

Celtic Spirituality
In this chapter on creation theology, I believe an authentic cre-

28. Thomas Berry, 1988, op. cit., page 11.
29. Patrick Kavanagh, *The Complete Poems*, (To a Child, 1972), Kavanagh Press, page 7.
30. *Veritatis Splendor*, The Catholic Truth Society, London, 1993.
31. *Evangelium Vitae*, No 6, Veritas Publications, Dublin, 1995.
32. Thavis, John, 'Environmental concerns go beyond Vatican's borders', *The Pittsburgh Catholic*, 11 November 1988, page 4.

ation spirituality would help regenerate Irish Christianity and especially Irish Catholicism. I take on board the caution of Tom O'Loughlin, who introduces a reflection on Celtic Spirituality by pointing out there is no homogeneity within the broad range of interests which invoke labels such as 'Celtic Spirituality' or 'Celtic Christianity'.[33] Celtic spirituality celebrated the goodness of God that was manifested in the beauty of the world around us. Though St Patrick did not write the prayer that is known as his Breastplate, it does reflect the positive evaluation of creation in natural elements. Creation is not merely good but God's presence can be found everywhere if we just have the eyes to see:

I bind unto myself today
The virtues of the star-lit heaven,
The glorious sun's life-giving ray,
The whiteness of the moon at even,
The flashing of the lightening free,
The whirling wind's tempestuous shocks,
The stable Earth, the deep salt sea
Around the old eternal rocks.

Many Celtic monasteries were sited in remote and beautiful places like Skellig and Iona. It is no wonder that the monks came to love the cry of the curlew, the flight of the gannet, the bark of seals, the beauty of trees and wild flowers and the buzzing of bees and insects. The Celtic church did not excoriate or attempt to eradicate the sensitivity towards creation that was present in the pre-Christian religious tradition. A well that had been a sacred site for the Druidic tradition became St Mary's well, and worship in many of these wells or holy places continues right into the 21st century.[34] Brigid's Abbey is known as *Cill Dara* (the church of the oak). On two crosses on the island of Iona dating

---

33. Thomas O'Loughlin, 'Celtic Spirituality, Ecumenism and the Contemporary Religious Landscape', *Irish Theological Quarterly*, Summer 2002, page 135.
34. Philip Newell, op. cit., page 27.

from the 9th century, St John's and St Martin's, we find art work where nature and scriptural presentations are intertwined.[35]

Other Irish saints are also well known for their love of nature. St Brendan of Clonfert (died 575) was a great seafarer. During their journeys, he and his monks befriended every creature they met from crustaceans to birds. They spent one Easter with a friendly whale.[36]

St Kevin of Glendalough (died 616) was also sensitive to the needs of other creatures. In a dark moment when he was tempted to destroy some of the forest and hills to build an elaborate monastery, he firmly resisted the temptation with these words:

> I have no wish that the creatures of God should be moved because of me: my God can help me find a place in some other fashion. And moreover, all the wild creatures on these mountains are my house mates, gentle and familiar to me, and they would be sad of this that thou hast said.[37]

Similar stories are told about St Colmcille. One story tells of a heron which the saint predicted would arrive on Iona from Ireland weary and exhausted. The saint instructed the young monk to look out for the bird and when it arrived, 'you will take heed to lift it tenderly and carry it to the house nearby, and having taken it as a guest there you will wait on it for three days and nights and feed it with anxious care'.[38]

St Columban was also renowned for his love of animals. Jonas, St Columban's biographer, describes Columban playing with his animal friends in the forest:

> Chagnoald, The Bishop of Laon, was once his secretary and disciple. He told me that he often saw him when he was praying or fasting in the wilderness. He used to call the wild beasts and birds, and they would come to him at once and he would fondle them tenderly with his hands; and they loved

35. Ibid., page 35.

36. Quoted in Edward Echlin's *The Christian Green Heritage*, Grove Books Limited, Bramcote, Nottingham NG9 3DS, 1989, page 7.

37. Ibid., page 7, taken from Helen Wadell's *Beasts and the Saints*, Constable, London, 1934, page 136.

38. Marian Keaney, *Irish Missionaries*, Veritas, Dublin, 1985, page 38.

to sport and play with him, as happy as puppies with their master. There is a little creature which people call the squirrel, and he would call it down from the topmost branches and take it in his hand and set it on his shoulder and it would creep in and out of his bosom; and the same witness said he often saw this happen.[39]

Having followed in the footsteps of St Columban in eastern France around Annegray and Luxeuil and Northern Italy in Bobbio in the summer of 2002, I saw that the natural world, especially unspoiled places like caves, had a special significance for him. Columban loved retiring to woods or caves to pray and be alone with God. It is natural that statues and artwork depicting St Columban in Europe in the 8th and 9th century often showed him with birds or small animals on his shoulders.

The best known Irish Christian in Europe in the 9th century was John Scotus Eriugena. He was also very convinced of God's presence in creation. His theology was shaped by the Johannine tradition. He taught that St John the Evangelist had listened attentively to the divine call, both in the Word and in all creation. He regarded the world as a theophany or manifestation of God. Dermot Morgan claims that for Eriugena: 'the whole created world is to be understood as unfolding within the Trinity, at no stage is creation to be seen as an alienation or separation of things from God ... Eriugena's God is not static but dynamic, manifesting, unfolding, and explicating himself in spirals of divine history.'[40] Eriugena waxed eloquently on God's presence in everything, including the rocks that appeared lifeless. The way to learn about God, according to Eriugena, was 'through the letters of scripture and through the species of creation'.[41]

Eriugena's most celebrated work is called *Periphyseon*

39. Desmond Forristal, *Columbanus*, Messenger Publications, Dublin, page 20.
40. Dermot Morgan, 'Nature, Man and God in the Philosophy of John Scotus Eriugena', in Richard Kearney (ed), *The Irish Mind*, Wolfhound Press, Dublin, 1985, pages 99-100.
41. Ibid., page 35; quoted in Philip Newell's *Listening for the Heartbeat of God*, page 35. Reference to John Scotus Eriugena, (translated by

(Division of Nature). In it he develops in a systematic way his belief in the essential goodness of creation. He claims that 'divine
goodness is the essence of the whole universe and its substance.'[42]
He insists that nothing in nature is evil as such, and that when we
sin we are acting contrary to our fundamental nature. Somewhat
like Pelagius before him, Eriugena taught that grace and nature
were not opposed but that grace co-operates with nature releas-
ing its essential goodness.[43] Because of his constant insistence on
the divine vivifying presence in all reality, Eriugena's thought
was condemned as pantheistic by the Pope. His writings were
placed on the Index (the list of forbidden books drawn up by the
Inquisition) in 1685. Once again, another potentially rich source
for presenting balanced Christian teaching about creation was
lost.

Irish monks developed nature poetry almost one thousand
years before similar poetry developed in other European ver-
nacular languages. One of the best known poems is by the monk
Marban who feels nurtured and protected by nature even in
solitude. He is content to live in the woods:

For I inhabit a wood
Unknown but to my God
My house of hazel and ash
As an old hut in a rath.

And my house small, but not too small,
Is always accessible:
Women disguised as blackbirds
Talk their words from the gable.

The stag erupts from rivers,
Brown mountains tell the distance:
I am glad as poor as this
Even in men's absence.

Christopher Bamford), *The Voice of the Eagle*, Lindisfarne Press, 1990,
Homily XI.
42. Ibid., 36. Reference to John Scotus Eriugena, (translated by John
O'Meara) *Periphyseon*, 1987, (6811).
43. Ibid., page 36.

Death-green of yew,
Huge green of oak
Sanctify,
And apples grow
Close by new nuts;
Water hides.

Young of things,
Bring faith to me,
Guard my door;
The rough, unloved,
Wild dogs, tall deer,
Quiet does.

In small tame bands
The badgers are,
Grey outside:
And foxes dance
Before my door
All the night.

All at evening
The day's first meal
Since dawn's bread:
 Trapped trout, sweet sloes
And honey, haws,
Beer and herbs.

Moans, movements of
Slivers-breasted
Birds rouse me:
Pigeons perhaps,
And the thrush sings
Constantly.

Black-winged beetles
Boom, and small bees;
November
Through the lone geese
A wild winter
Music stirs.

Come fine white gulls
All sea-singing
And less sad,
Lost in heather,
The grouse's song
Little sad.

For music I
Have pines, my tall
Music-pines
So who can I
Envy here, my
Gentle Christ.[44]

Love of nature and an ability to find God there lives on in
modern Irish poetry. Patrick Kavanagh's poem ,'The One' cap-
tures that special sense of God that comes to us in the few areas
of relative wilderness that survive in modern Ireland:
    Green, blue, yellow and red –
    God is down in the swamps and marshes
    Sensational as April and almost incred-
        ible the flowering of our catharsis.
    A humble scene in a backward place
    Where no one important ever looked
    The raving flower looked up in the face
    Of the One and the Endless, the Mind that baulked
    The profoundest of mortals. A primrose, a violet,
    A violent wild iris – but mostly the anonymous performers

---

44. John Montague (ed.), *The Faber Book of Irish Verse*, Faber and Faber,
London, 1974, pages 57-58.

Yet an important occasion as the Muse at her toilet
Prepared to inform the local farmers
That beautiful, beautiful, beautiful God
Was breathing His love by a cut-away bog.

Among contemporary Irish poets, the work of Michael Longley is also imbued through and through with a comprehensive knowledge, love and fascination with nature, particularly in the West of Ireland. Many of his poems dwell on the landscape of Ireland and a variety of creatures that inhabit this space with us humans. Often, as in 'The Ice-Cream-Man', Longley contrasts the senseless violence of murdering an ice-cream man in Belfast with the beauty of nature in the Burren. The counterpoint is between the ice-cream man's chant – 'Rum and raisin, vanilla, butter-scotch, walnut, peach' and a litany of the wild flowers which he saw in a single day in the Burren. These include 'Meadowsweet, tway blade, crowfoot, ling, angelica, herb robert, marjoram, cow parsley, sundew, vetch, mountain avens, wood sage, ragged robin, stitchwort, yarrow, lady's bedstraw, bindweed, bog pimpernel'.

That same knowledge and love of nature burst forth again in 'Carrigskeewaun'. This poem is rooted in a very special place in County Mayo. Longley acknowledges that 'Carrigskeewaun is unbelievably beautiful, it's the most magical place in the world for me. It's the Garden of Eden and I often think about it. If I am depressed, I go for a walk in my mind up the path to the cottage around the little ruined outhouses and I stand taking in the view, even though I am in Belfast or London or New York.'[45] The poem shows that he is equally at home with the bird life of the west of Ireland as with the plant life.

In 'Osprey', 'The White Butterfly', 'Water-Lily', 'The Lapwing', 'The Seal', 'The Daffodils', 'The Rabbit', Longley's keen and accurate observations about nature are used as 'emblems for his own imaginative engagement with the world'.[46] Liam Heaney

45. www.bbc.co.uk/northernireland/poetry/nature1.shtml, Carrigskeewaun, page 2 of 3, 19/04/03.
46. Liam Heaney, 'Natural Perceptions: The Poetry of Michael Longley', *Studies*, Summer 2002, page 179.

ends his article on Longley's poetry in the magazine *Studies*, by observing that 'Nature is the means whereby he, as poet, is empowered to unfold the complex phenomena of the natural and physical world. This affords Longley's poetry a universal significance and an explicit ecological dimension.'[47]

In 'Badger' Longley again shows his intimate knowledge of this creature. In the first section of the poem he locates the badger at the heart of pre-Christian mythology – 'between cromlech and stone circle'. His sympathy is with the animal, both from the way he contrasts the digging skills of the fox and hare and the description of the badger's intestine and heel and head. He is acutely aware of the ambivalence which many Irish rural people have towards badgers. Because many people blame the badger for spreading tuberculosis among cattle, there is a price on the head of the badger. 'A head with a price on it.' Section 3 of the poem describes the death of the badger.[48]

In an article in the magazine *WildIreland*, Billy Flynn states that 'few wildlife issues in this country are as emotive as this one. Many farmers blame badgers alone for TB, while many conservationists deny any link between badgers and the disease because the evidence for the transfer of the disease from badgers is largely circumstantial.'[49]

In the body of the article, Flynn goes on to point out that very often farmers and the Department of Agriculture overlook the fact that TB in a herd is mainly passed on from cattle-to-cattle, especially when there is overcrowding on farms. Badgers were TB free until the 1960s. In the past 40 years there has been almost a 100% increase in the number of cattle in Ireland, up from 4,683,700 in 1960 to 7,097,430 in 2001.[50] Maybe we should be asking whether this level of stocking is too intensive for a country like Ireland, with our particular climate, soil texture and waterways.

47. Ibid., page 181.
48. www.teachnet.ie/ekelly/badger.html, page 1.
49. Billy Flynn, 'Badgers and bovine TB – an introduction', *WildIreland*, January/February, pages 9-11.
50. Ibid., page 10.

Flynn also points out that the culling programme, which is favoured by the Department of Agriculture, could very well lead to the extinction of our native badger stock. By supporting culling, the Irish Government is in breach of many wild life conventions, including the Convention on the Conservation of European Wildlife and Natural Habitats. Badgers are protected by this treaty.

Martyrs for Life
The Christian churches have always celebrated the lives of women and men who have given their lives for the faith. Today Christians should honour those who have given time, expertise and sometimes their lives to promote biodiversity. One example is particularly instructive and poignant. Nikolai Vivilov was born in Moscow in 1887. He trained as a biologist and by the 1920s was working at the All Union Institute of Applied Botany in St Petersburg. He organised expeditions to gather seeds from all over the Soviet Union, Iran, Ethiopia, Mexico, Afghanistan, Pakistan and Japan and about 50 other countries. Unfortunately he fell foul of the geneticist Lysenko, who denounced him at a genetics conference in 1937. This ended his brilliant career. He was arrested on a trumped up-charge of being a 'British spy' in 1940 and he is thought to have died in a Siberian concentration camp.[51] Before that tragic event, Vavilov and his collaborators had assembled a comprehensive picture of global agro-diversity in 400 institutes across the Soviet Union. Tens of thousands of crop species were collected and classified. His wheat collection included 26,000 varieties.

In 1942, at the height of World War II, the German army laid siege to the city of St Petersburg (then named Leningrad) and cut off the food supply. It was a horrendous few months during which 600,000 people died from hunger, starvation and disease.

---

51. Trofim Lysenko (1898–1976) is notorious in the field of genetics. When he found his communist ideology was challenged by Mendel's laws of genetics, instead of abandoning his belief that heredity could be changed by good husbandry, he denounced Mendelian genetics and banished many outstanding Soviet biologists and geneticists.

During the siege, hungry Russian scientists remained at the Institute protecting the vast collection of seeds from rats and the elements. In all, fourteen scientists died of starvation surrounded by these bags of seed. They could have eaten the seeds to save their lives. Instead they were willing to sacrifice their lives so that rare seeds would be available to future generations. We must honour their memory by doing everything we can to preserve different species around the globe.[52]

Chico Mendes (1944-1988)

In the later part of the 20th century, many people gave their lives to protect God's creation. The best known is probably Chico Mendes. He grew up in a family of rubber trappers in the Amazon area of Brazil. Rubber trappers had extracted the rubber sap from trees in the tropical forest without destroying the forest. However, in the 1970s and 1980s, cattle ranchers and mining groups moved into that Amazon area. They cut and burned the forest and left behind land that can be grazed for a few years before the soil is eroded and it becomes a waste land. Mendes tried to organise the rubber trappers (known locally as *seringueiros*) to protest against the destruction of the Amazon. He paid dearly for his activism. He was gaoled and fined on a number of occasions. Finally, on 22 December 1988, Chico Mendes was murdered. His death led to a huge international outcry against the destruction of tropical forests.

In the Philippines, Fr Karl Schmitz CP, a colleague of mine, ministered among the B'baan tribe in South Cotabato. He preached constantly against the destruction of the tropical forest in tribal lands. In 1988 he was murdered by an assassin who had been hired by a local logging group. Further north, Fr Mario 'Mark' Estorba was shot and killed in Butuan city in July 1988. He had furnished the civil authority with documentary evidence of atrocities committed by logging companies against local settlers and the tribal people of the region.

---

52. Belden C. Lane, 'Biodiversity and the Trinity', *America*, 17 December 2001, page 11.

Three years later, in October 1991, Fr Nerelito Satur was ambushed by gunmen hired by loggers in the province of Bukidnon in Mindanao. I knew Fr Satur well and had conducted an environmental seminar in Bukidnon in 1990, the year before he was killed.

CHAPTER 6

The Need for an Appropriate Ethical Framework

The task of humankind is not simply to create a world that is good for us, but to arrange this Earth to accommodate our own reasonable needs and those of our fellow creatures, or at least a good proportion of them, as long as the future lasts.
— Colin Tudge, *The Variety of Life*, page 609

In addition to creating an ecologically sensitive theology, the churches must develop an appropriate ethical framework for promoting the integrity of creation and justice especially in the light of the massive extinction that we are witnessing. The biologist Professor Edward O. Wilson has explained the importance of biodiversity from a biological perspective. In his writings, he emphasises the importance of each species in its own right and also the importance of maintaining the richness of biodiversity for the benefit of the biosphere and the human community. In more recent writing, he has highlighted the importance of protecting the earth from a moral perspective. 'Science and technology are what we can do; morality is what we agree we should or should not do.'[1] An adequate ethical system to deal with this current issue will demand a major shift away from the exclusively human or homocentric focus, which has been so pervasive in western ethics and in the wider cultural tradition.

As was the case with our theological tradition, western moral theology and ethics were also human centred. This anthropocentric ancestry has deeper roots in western thought, going back to the Greek dichotomy between matter and spirit. It is also present to a lesser extent in the Hebrew world. The biblical tradition was interpreted as affirming that humans were radically different from any other being or thing in creation. Humans alone

---

1. Wilson, op. cit., page 130.

were endowed with spirit which links them to God (Gen 1:26) rather than to other creatures. Only humans had intrinsic value because they were made in the image and likeness of God. Everything else in the world was there for our use and therefore only had instrumental value.

Since the 16th century, the writings of scientists like Francis Bacon, René Descartes and Isaac Newton, and philosophers like Hobbes, Locke and Jeremy Bentham, have further intensified this human-centred focus. In the succeeding centuries science, and its handmaiden technology, was viewed as a tool in the hands of human beings giving them power to dominate and manipulate the earth in whatever way they saw fit in order to secure human well-being and betterment.

Seeing that there is an almost unbridgeable chasm between humans and the rest of creation, it is understandable that nature was not endowed with a moral or sacred dimension. Nature was there to be dominated, shaped, used. Even abusing nature did not, in most cases, prompt moral sanctions. The utilitarian ethics which governed much individual and societal response to the natural world found few, if any, moral precepts to guide and structure the interaction between humans and the rest of creation. Humans could change and transform the natural world in the most extensive way, by cutting down forests or polluting water or the atmosphere, without feeling that they had transgressed any moral precept.

Any adequate ethical framework for dealing with these moral predicaments in the area of ecology must be based on our contemporary understanding of the relationship between humans and the rest of the natural world. Our evolutionary history makes it very clear that humans are not separate from the rest of nature. Rather, we are an integral part of the community of living beings and non-living reality. Each of us depends on the well-being of the whole and so we have to have respect for the community of living beings, for people, animals, plants and for the preservation of earth, water and soils.

Fr Thomas Berry feels that contemporary ethics must focus

its concerns on the larger community of the living. He states that:

> the human community is subordinate to the ecological community. The ecological imperative is not derived from human ethics. Human ethics is derivative from the ecological imperative. The primary ethical norm is the well-being of the comprehensive community, not the well-being of the human community. The earth is a single ethical system, as the universe is a single ethical system.[2]

This is the first principle of an ecological ethic. Such an ethic would demand a legal framework where the rights of the geological and biological, as well as the human, component of the earth community would be protected.

Ethical principles, drawn from the wider biocentric and theocentric framework, could underpin a very different approach to the natural world. They affirm that each creature, and especially every species, has intrinsic though not absolute value. The reason for this is that they are created by God and loved by him. Ecosystems have a particular value in keeping the biosphere stable and open to the conserving and transforming power of the Spirit through evolutionary processes. The morality of logging a tropical forest would appear different, depending on whether one was working from a utilitarian, or theocentric perspective. The utilitarian approach views the forest as merely resources to be exploited by humans for their benefit. The same action appears to take on a completely different moral hue when viewed from a theocentric perspective. All the creatures in the forest have intrinsic value and the ecosystem itself has intrinsic value. If the logging operation leads to the destruction of species, the erosion of topsoil and the destruction of the culture of tribal people, who have lived in harmony with the forest for generations, then the action is construed as morally repugnant. This has happened in the Philippines and, unfortunately, is still happening in Brazil and New Guinea today.

---

2. Berry, Thomas, 1994, 'Ethics and Ecology' unpublished paper.

An ecocentric ethical framework ought to incorporate the need for justice and equity in the use and distribution of the earth's resources among the human community. This basic Catholic moral principle, which is often, in its classical formulation, presented in a homocentric way, can easily be expanded to cover the wider earth community. The principle states that the goods of this world are meant for the benefit of all the creatures, and especially the peoples, of the world and not just a small segment of humankind living today.

People like ourselves living in the North must recognise that most of the ecological problems in our world today, from global warming to the destruction of the forest, stem from the impact which Northern affluence makes on the environment. Responding to them calls for a much more frugal way of living for the majority of people in First World countries and the elite in the Third World. The one billion people who live on less than one dollar a day, and may have to get by on a single meal, need to have more equitable access to the resources of the world to meet their basic needs.

In the words of the ethicist, Henry Shue, there is a need to distinguish between the 'subsistence' utilisation of the natural world by the poor in the Third World and elsewhere, and the 'luxury' use by many Northerners and the Third World elite. One must go even further and say that it is important to recognise the difference between 'life-enhancing products' like food production, and 'death-dealing' ones like the global arms trade and the traffic in illegal drugs. Those involved in these activities, or in the luxurious misuse of the global commons, bear much greater moral responsibility for the destruction of the forest and other natural resources than the majority of Third World people, and especially the forest dwellers.

In the light of the above it would appear that a fundamental requirement of any development strategy would be that it is ecologically sustainable and people-oriented. Let me spell out briefly what this might mean. Such development must be founded on a just national and international economic order where priority is given to the needs of the world's poor; it also must encourage people to actively participate in the decisions which affect their own lives by respecting the principle of subsidiarity. This principle envisages global institutions working in service of local and national ones. It would devise a way of promoting sustainable forestry by ensuring that forest management strategies follow the ecological cycle rather than the shorter financial cycle. This way, true value would be given to protecting biodiversity.

Another way to approach moral reality is to approach it from a 'rights' perspective. The German theologian Jürgen Moltmann takes such an approach. He begins his reflection by stating that the notion of human rights is now accepted almost universally. According to him, 'human rights are increasingly going to provide the universally valid, ethical framework for the evaluation and legitimation of 'human' policy.'[3] But for Moltmann, the human rights of individuals must be seen within the wider parameters of social rights.

The Rights of Future Generations

Among the social rights are the rights of future generations. Traditional ethical concerns normally dealt with the impact of behaviour on individuals or communities in the here-and-now or, at the most, the immediate future. Moltmann would consider that the laws of inheritance were a kind of contract between the generations. That is no longer an adequate framework because this generation is bringing about such massive changes to the fabric of the earth. The moral question is simple: Does this generation have the right to use up all the fossil fuel in the world, erode its topsoil, deplete the ozone layer, build up nuclear waste and destroy tropical forest in order to enable a fifth of the world's population to live in affluence? This principle states that future generations have the right to inherit a world as fertile and beautiful as the world this generation inhabits. This applies es-

---

3. Jürgen Moltmann, 'Human Rights, The Rights of Humanity and the Rights of Nature', in *The Ethics of World Religions and Human Rights*, *Concilium*, April 1990, SCM Press, London, pages 120 -134.

pecially in the area of protecting biodiversity and the natural systems of the planet, like the ozone layer, which are at present under attack from human activity.

Moltmann also argues that there cannot be human rights without the rights of the earth. Other creatures have more than just utility value for us. There is a need to articulate the rights of other living beings and the rights of the earth itself. As human dignity is the source for human rights, 'the dignity of creation is the source of natural rights of other living beings on the earth.'[4] These rights need to be articulated in law. Moltmann believes that the special dignity of human beings made in the image and likeness of God does not give a licence to exploit other living creatures. On the contrary, 'as images of the Creator, human beings love all their fellow creatures with the Creator's love'.[5]

Thoughout this book, I have shared the growing concerns of scientists that the stress created by people in First World countries will have a huge negative impact on the well-being of the planet within 40 or 50 years. Their warnings have been augmented by computer models which the authors of *Limits to Growth* have run during the past 30 years. In these models the analysts include environmental, economic and social data like demography. While in 1972 they found that the human footprints were within the carrying capacity of the planet at that time, by 1992 the growth of human activity had overshot the planet's resources, both on the resource side and the sink side of the equation. The latter refers to the ability of the earth to absorb human-generated pollution without doing serious, irreparable damage. Their recent book, *2004*, using updates from the same computer model, predicts that if our footprints continue to rise exponentially this will lead to the collapse of many of the support systems of the planet – air, water, fertile soils and forests – within 40 years. This is not inevitable, but to reach a sustainable future humanity must increase the consumption levels of the world's poor, while at the same time reducing humanity's total

---

4. Ibid., pages 131 and 132.
5. Ibid., pages 132-133.

ecological footprint.[6] Turning around a global growth-oriented economy will take enormous resources and human effort locally, nationally and globally. Unfortunately, the vast number of political, economic or religious leaders are not responding to the planet's huge environmental problems as quickly as they should. Every year that is lost will mean enormous suffering for many people in just 30 or 40 years' time. There is also the fear that the scale of the damage is so great that we may not be able to stem the tide of destruction.

6. Donella Meadows, Jorgen Randers, Dennis Meadows, op. cit., xv.

CHAPTER 7

Called to Live Lightly on the Earth

The idea that there might be limits to growth is for many people impossible to imagine. Limits are politically unmentionable and economically unthinkable. The culture tends to deny the possibility of limits by placing a profound faith in the powers of technology, the workings of the free market, and the growth of the economy as the solution to all problems, even problems created by growth.
— Meadows, Randers and Meadows,
Limits to Growth: The 30 Year Update, page 203

How happy are the poor in spirit,
Theirs is the kingdom of heaven. — Matthew 5:3

Following on from the last chapter is the insight that at the heart of an earth-centred spirituality or ethic is the need both to live more lightly on the earth and to work for a more just and equitable human community. The One Earth Community puts it as follows: 'Lifestyles of high material consumption must yield to the provision of greater sufficiency for all. For the rest of the world to reach United States levels of consumption with existing technologies would require four more planets Earth.'[1]

Everyone will admit that greed, covetousness and other commonly recognised human vices have undoubtedly contributed to our present crisis. Nevertheless, the principal cause of ecological devastation in our world today has been the unrelenting pursuit of what many people consider a good and desirable thing – the modern, growth-oriented, industrial model of development. What many people feel is the good life, something to be aspired to and worked for, is in fact destroying the world. The fundamental dynamic of the market economy promotes con-

---

1. Edward O. Wilson, *The Future of Life*, op. cit., page 150.

stant economic growth and short lifespan for goods so that more
and more products can be forced through the market economy.
This involves accumulating wealth and promoting high levels of
consumption. But it is impossible to have constant growth on a
finite planet.

Even scientists can be deluded into thinking that planet earth
has infinite resources and also an infinite capacity to absorb the
waste products of our industrial process. *The Guardian* corres-
pondent George Monbiot made a telling point in this area some
years ago. He was reflecting on comments by the Princeton
physicist, Freeman Dyson, that the planet Mars could be made
habitable within the next 50 years by planting genetically engineered trees. The Princeton professor argued this could facilitate
space tourism and encourage the export of 'surplus population'
to protect the earth from ecological disaster. As Monbiot points
out, 'his plan threatens to precipitate the very catastrophe he
wants to avoid', namely the destruction of this world.[2]

Scientists and former astronauts are still promoting the idea
of colonising the moon and Mars. In an article in the *National
Geographic*, Harrison H. Schmitt, the last astronaut to walk on
the moon in 1972, is now calling for a return of the Apollo programme to promote the colonisation of places in the solar system, like the moon and Mars. Such a programme would also
boost lunar tourism which would cost a mere $200,000 per per-
son. Once again, Schmitt does not advert to the financial and resource cost of such initiatives. He likens this space initiative to
homo sapiens breaking out of Africa 80,000 years ago. The fact
that the moon has no atmosphere and that food cannot be grown
there without enormous costs does not seem to have crossed his
mind. Like a true technophiliac, he has a naïve belief that technology will solve every problem.[3]

The $1 trillion that President George Bush has earmarked for
a manned trip to Mars could be much better spent on social and

2. George Monbiot, 'Beware of the appliance of Science', *The Guardian*,
24 February 2000, page 22.
3. Harrison H. Schmitt, 'My Seven', *National Geographic*, July 2004.

ecological projects here on earth. In the US itself the money ear-
marked for Mars would pay the salaries of an extra 1,103,925
grade school teachers. It would make available $300 per year for
every one of the 48 million Aids sufferers for the next 60 years.
On the ecological front, the President could spend $400 billion
which it would cost the US to implement the Kyoto Protocol on
fossil fuel emissions. This would leave plenty of money to fund
the development of alternative sources of energy.[4] Some of this
money might also be used to meet the poverty reduction
millennium goals which promised to halve the number of people
living in extreme poverty by 2015. The cost of such initiative is
estimated to be about $50 billion per annum on top of the $50 billion in current aid programmes.

Living with limits

Humans, especially westerners, have lived so long in a world
where frontiers could be continuously breached. When one
habitat was destroyed or resources used up, humans simply
moved on to a new frontier. This frontier mentality has particularly marked the popular culture of the United States. It was a
crucial factor in opening up the prairies and moving many people to the west coast in the 19th century. The problem today is
that there are no new frontiers, and yet we are consuming the
world as if there were.

In 1986 a study by Peter Vitousek *et al* estimated that humans
have now captured 40% of terrestrial energy for their own exclusive use. If one includes the oceans. the percentage drops to
25%.[5] This leaves only 60% for improving the lives of three quar-
ters of the world's population and for the needs of all the other
creatures who share this planet with us. This finding is extremely
important as it sets the context for the optimum scale of human

4. 'Charlotte Denny and Charlotte Moore on how George Bush could
have used the money spent of the mission to Mars', *The Guardian*, 21
January 2004, supplement, page 13.
5. P. Vitousek, P.M. Ehrlich, P. R. Ehrlich, A.H. Matson, 'Human
Appropriation of the Products of Photosynthesis', *Bioscience*, Vol 34, No
6, pages 368-373.

activity, including economic activity, in relation to the needs of other creatures on earth. The call for a five-fold increase in worldwide economic activity contained in the book *Our Common Future*, appears totally unrealistic if Vitousek and his collaborators are at all close to the mark.

Possible constraints on economic growth had previously been discussed in the book *Limits to Growth*, which was published in 1972. At that point it seemed that human population levels and the impact of human economic activity was comfortably below the planet's carrying capacity.[6] The book recommended that humans reduce their demands on the planet across a range of human activities. It became a bestseller and led to a wide ranging debate about the relationship between economic activity and the local and global environment's ability to cope. It discussed both the resource base of our planet and its ability to cope with human activity. This is known as the sink base. The book was translated into about 30 languages. Authors such as Herman Kahn, Julian Simon dismissed the conclusions of the study as inaccurate and pessimistic. They argued that human inventiveness and technology would enable economic growth to continue almost indefinitely. Economics and politics for the past three decades have operated on the premise that the limits to growth perspective was false. Unfortunately, we are now living beyond the carrying capacity of the planet but very few people in the western world are aware of it. The only time limits cross their minds is when oil prices surge upwards. Even then they expect them to decline when the current political or economic crisis passes.

The authors of *Limits to Growth* updated their study in 1992 in a book called *Beyond the Limits*. It confirmed most of the predictions in the earlier work but warned that humanity had already overshot the limits of the Earth's support capacity.[7] They claimed

---

6. Donella Meadows, Jorgen Randers, Dennis Meadows, *Limits to Growth: the 30 Year Update*, Chelsea Green Publishing Company, White River Junction, Vermont, 2004, page xii.
7. Ibid., pages XII-XIII. Summary given in preface.

that, for example, *per capita* grain production peaked around the mid-1980s. The prospects of extra fish production from the ocean is no longer possible despite improved technology, and the availability of fresh water for human consumption and agriculture is becoming a problem in many areas.

In order to make us much more sensitive to the fact that we are living in a finite world, and that currently we have breached its capacity to sustain our demands, we need to develop a more adequate accounting system. The normal economic indices, which we hear and see constantly in the media, like the growth in gross national product (GNP), or the rise and fall of shares on the stock market, or the consumer price index, tell us little about what is actually happening to the poor of the planet and the planet itself.

Mathis Wackernagel and his colleagues set about developing a new measure which would calculate the impact that human beings are having on the planet. They called it the 'human eco-logical footprint' which they defined as the land area that would be required to provide the resources (grain, food, wood, fish and urban land) and absorb the emissions (carbon dioxide) for the global society.[8] According to this measure, global society had overshot our ecological footprint by 20% in 1990 and we have continued this upward curve ever since, even though well over two billion people live in misery.

A number of years ago *Friends of the Earth* in the Netherlands tried to apply a similar accounting system in Holland. It as-sessed what the allowable level of consumption of environmen-tal resources would be for the average Dutch person in the year 2010, if resource levels were equal for each person on the planet, and if the resources were to be used in a sustainable way. In one key area, the use of fossil fuel, the researchers found that, at the time, *per capita* carbon dioxide levels stood at 12 tons in the Netherlands. This would need to be reduced to 4 tons by 2010. Within these restrictions the average Dutch person could chose between travelling 15.5 miles by car, 31 miles by bus, 40 miles by

8. Ibid., page xiv.

train or 6.2 by plane each day. Much of modern global tourism would collapse as individuals could only fly from Amsterdam to Rio de Janeiro once every 20 years if such an accounting system was introduced.

Dr Rowan Williams, Archbishop of Canterbury, has backed a similar initiative called the Global Commons Institute plan for a fair sharing of fossil fuel use between countries. It is known as the 'contraction and convergence' policy and involves every person on the planet having an equal right and quota to emit carbon dioxide. He explains that in the first 48 hours of 2004 the average US family would be responsible for the emission of as much carbon dioxide as a Tanzanian family would in the whole year.[9] The fastest growing source of carbon dioxide growth in Britain is transport. Emissions increased by 50% between 1990 and 2002. Flying accounts for most of this, but another reason is the huge increase in 4x4s vehicles. British people buy 150,000 such vehicles each year, not for haulage tasks on farms but merely for driving around the cities. In the US such vehicles, which are subsidised through tax breaks, now account for 46% of the private fleet.[10]

Similar accounting systems should be developed to assess humanity's impact on other creatures so that effective policies can be developed to conserve the diversity of species globally. A few years ago, experts calculated that humans are taking half the available fresh water on the planet. This leaves the other half to all the rest of creation.[11] More and more one species, *homo sapiens*, is cornering all the resources of the planet and thereby denying these to other species. No wonder then that they are being pushed into oblivion.

The challenge today is to raise the standard of living of the poor while, at the same time, reducing human pressure on the planet. To achieve this we would need to lower population, alter

9. Paul Brown, 'Climate change threatens species, says archbishop', *The Guardian*, 6 July 2004, page 9.
10. George Monbiot, 'Driving into the Abyss', *The Guardian*, 6 July 2004, page 21.
11. *Now, It's Not Personal!*, op. cit., page 14.

consumption levels and promote more resource-efficient technologies. All of this will only be possible with concerted political
will at local and global level. Computer models used by the authors of *Limits to Growth: The 30-Year Update* project that 8 billion
people could live at levels of well-being similar to the lower in-
come rates of present day Europe if we make the necessary
changes during the next decade or so.[12] One thing is clear: a future
with constant economic growth is a pipedream in a finite planet.

The use of indices like ecological footprints and the Living
Planet Index will teach us that western affluent people have
much to learn from tribal societies that are able to live more or
less in harmony with their environment. The T'boli people of
South Cotabato in the Philippines, with whom I lived for 12
years, lived lightly on the earth. They used the forest for over a
thousand years but did not consume it or diminish its diversity.
The forest has provided them with food, clothing, building material, medicines, and artistic and spiritual inspiration. What we
learn from them can help us abandon our materialistic view of
the world, especially our over-use of energy and our wasteful
use of the earth's limited resources.

We need to change radically and develop a new respect for
all life, to see it as precious and ultimately mysterious. This is
clear even to a biologist like Edward Wilson. Recently he wrote
that 'Without mystery, life shrinks'.[13] Christians who believe
that Jesus came so that all 'may have life and have it to the full'
(Jn 10:10) should be in the forefront of any campaign to protect
life locally and globally.

Heavy Human Footprints on the Planet
I wonder is it possible that the Catholic position on birth control,
as enunciated in *Humanae Vitae*, might be one of the reasons why
the Catholic Church has been so slow to enter this debate and
the wider ecological debate. One of the principal causes of environmental degradation and extinction is both the growth in the

12. Donella Meadows, Jorgen Randers, Dennis Meadows, *Limits to
Growth: the 30 Year Update*, op. cit., page xii.
13. Edward O. Wilson, *The Future of Life*, op. cit., page 11.

human population and more, specifically, the growth in human demands on the planet as more and more people aspire to a western, affluent life style.

World population has been growing exponentially since the beginning of the industrial revolution. For example, in 1650 there were only 500 million people on the whole planet. It took a century and a half for the number to reach one billion in 1800. In 1965 population reached 3.3 billion. This has almost doubled to over 6 billion over the past 40 years and the numbers are still rising.

I explored the population issues in greater detail in my book *The Greening of the Church* where I made the point that the earth's carrying capacity for different levels of population was not addressed in the encyclical *Humanae Vitae*. Today, when measuring tools like the human ecological footprint are available both in bioregions and globally, there is an urgent need to revisit the population issue. It is important to state that a fall in population levels will not, of itself, reduce the stress on the planet unless it is accompanied by a drop in our consumption patterns. Nevertheless, the time is now ripe for the Catholic Church to revisit its teaching on birth control.[14] The basis of that teaching is that each act of sexual intercourse must be open to life. But if this leads, as it inevitably must, to larger families, then there will be an increased stress on global ecosystems which could trigger a major collapse of global ecosystems within four or five decades. Such a breakdown, especially in the area of food production, will lead to a dramatic fall in human population levels which may well be permanent because the damage done to the earth's fertility could be irreversible.

The irony then would be that a strict adherence to *Humanae Vitae*, which sets out to promote respect for life, could in the longer term undermine the conditions which are necessary for human life in the future. An ecological ethical perspective must focus on reality in a holistic way rather than on the interaction of

14. Seán McDonagh, *The Greening of the Church*, Chapter 2, Chapman, London, 1990.

any individual entities or actors. We know that, if we are to protect other creatures from extinction, we have to show much
greater generosity in sharing the global commons with them. At
the moment, our economic and political culture assumes that all
the global space – on land, in the air and the seas – primarily be-
longs to humans. That assumption also underpinned *Humanae
Vitae*

Our human space is now encroaching on the space of every
other creature on the planet. As we saw in Chapter 2, without
adequate space creatures are forced into extinction and the
whole body of creation is affected and diminished. Even in the
first account of Creation in Genesis we see God making provision for all creatures, not just humans. Now we know that these
kinds of provisions have to be made on a finite planet. An ethic
which flows from this perspective challenges us to evaluate individual choices, like having more and more children, in the
context of its impact on all creation. This interaction between individual acts and their repercussions for the planet is now a new
ethical context for many human actions, be it in the area of consumption, economics or demography. As Cho Hyun-Chul
writes, 'sin is a rejection of the ecological unity that we are related to nature in the organic body of the world. We [human be-
ings] must stay in our space so that other creatures, to which we
are inseparably related and on which we are fundamentally dependent, may get space for existence and life and thus thrive.
Only then can we too continue to exist, live and flourish.[15]

The dangers posed by excessive population are not just about
the number of people living in the country or on the Earth. It
also includes their level of affluence, energy use and demand for
resources. In 1990 the World Food Program at Brown University
calculated that if the world food harvest over the previous few
years was distributed equitably to the all the people of the
world, it could provide a vegetarian diet for 6 billion people. In
contrast, a meat-rich diet, favoured by affluent countries and
currently available to the global elite, could only manage to feed

15. Cho, Hyun-Chul SJ, op. cit., page 260.

2.6 billion. Human society is increasingly going to be faced with the option of getting its protein from animals or plants. If we opt for animals it will mean a more inequitable world with increasing levels of human misery.[16] The tragedy is that other countries, as they become richer, are adopting the western meat-rich diet. In 1960, for example, Mexico only fed 5% of its grain harvest to animals. By 2004 the figure has climbed to 45%. Similarly, Egypt has gone from 3% to 31% in the same period. Most worrying of all China, which has one sixth of the world's population, has gone from feeding 8% of its grain to animals to 26% in 40 years. In all of these countries the poor could use this grain to stave off malnutrition, improve their health and well-being, but they cannot afford it.[17] Another reason for promoting a low-meat diet is that finding water to grow food for the 8 billion people who will be living on the planet by 2020 is one of the major problems facing governments. Even at the moment, groundwater levels are plummeting and rivers are overstressed, according to a report from the International Water Management Institute (IWMI).[18] The report confirms that meat-eaters consume the equivalent of 5,000 litres (1,100 gallons) of water each day compared with the 1,000-2,000 consumed by those who mostly eat grain and vegetables. On average, it takes 1,790 litres of water to grow 1kg of wheat compared to 9,680 litres for 1kg of beef.[19]

The Christian churches should be promoting a more vegetarian diet because of its implications for making more food available for hungry people and for protecting vital agricultural land and water sources.

Our Faith calls today for simple living.
It is obvious that, if future generations are to share in a planet as beautiful and fertile as the one this generation shares we will have to live more simply. All religious traditions have encouraged

16. *Now, It's Not Personal!*, op. cit., page 13.
17. Richard Manning, 'The Oil We Eat', *Harper's Magazine*, February 2004, page 45.
18. John Vidal, 'Meat-eaters soak up the world's water', *The Guardian*, 23 August 2004, page10.
19. Ibid.

their followers to live in simple way and not to become attached
to either power or money, because these have a way of diverting
our hearts from what is most important in life. This call for
moderation in our lifestyle is particularly significant today. It
arises from the simple fact that the majority of people will not be
able to meet their basic needs for food, clothing and shelter if a
small segment of humans sequester the lion's share of the
earth's resources. Furthermore, such a way of living is impairing
the ability of the planet to sustain future generations at a level
that they will need to meet their basic needs.

So the Christian challenge to promote moderation today arises
from concerns for social justice and the integrity of God's creation. *The Catechism of the Catholic Church* teaches that God calls
humans to share in his providence towards other creatures,
which involves a responsibility for the world which God has en-
trusted to them.[20] The contemporary expression of that calls for
all Christians to live more simply. This will not be easy. We live
in a world of all-pervasive advertising which directly and indi-
rectly tells people that they are important and of value if they
wear the best clothes, drive top-of-the-range cars, live in luxurious houses and have at least one other house somewhere in a
warmer climate. Advertising is telling people that they are what
they own or wear. St Francis' great love for other creatures – his
brothers and sisters – flowed from his freely chosen poverty
which freed him from enslavement or undue attachment to possessions. He saw himself imitating Jesus who possessed nothing
and yet gave himself to everyone (Mk 10:17-22).

Ireland has seen unprecedented levels of prosperity during
the past decade. On the positive side, this new found wealth has
created employment opportunities for young people so that
they no longer have to emigrate like previous generations. On
the negative side is the extraordinary growth in materialism in a
short time, despite the fact that many people still consider themselves Christian. Sadly, there has been little leadership from political or religious leaders to challenge people about succumbing

20. *The Catechism of the Catholic Church*, Veritas, Dublin, 1994, No 373.

to the lure of money and possessions. Very few voices are promoting frugality as a human and Christian option today. The current level of wealth and use of the earth's resources cannot be shared equally by all the people on the planet, so it is inherently unjust to others. It is also unsustainable and so is unjust to future generations of humans and other creatures. To make a conscious choice to live more frugally will call for new networks of support from the Christian community where moderation, care and solidarity will be valued above money and property.

The Australian bishops have shown leadership in tackling environmental problems from a justice and faith standpoint. Their 2002 social justice statement, *A New Earth: The Environmental Challenge,* is an attractive publication and it engages local and global environmental challenges. It takes St Francis's *Canticle of Brother Sun* and reflects on what is happening to land, water and air. The bishops make suggestions on the ways in which individuals, community groups, politicians and public servants might respond to the environmental crisis. The social justice document was accompanied by an environmental video in which individual bishops endorsed the letter's message and called on Catholics to see environmental challenges as moral and religious ones. Finally, they set up an Earth Care Council to advise the bishops on what can often be complex environmental challenges.

Two years later, the Catholic bishops of Victoria and South Australia have written a pastoral letter on the problems facing the Murray Darling river. This document elaborates on the social justice statement which stated that: 'The health of the Murray-Darling Basin epitomises the ecological crisis. This once great waterway now surrenders 80% of its flow for human consumption. Since the European settlement, between 12 and 15 billion trees have been lost from the Basin. The river system, which is a major artery of Australia's agriculture, is exhausted and dying. Because of water removal or irrigation, the river at times does not have the strength to reach the sea.'

In August 2004, the Bishops of Queensland wrote a pastoral

on the dangers facing the Great Barrier Reef which runs for 2,000 kilometres down the eastern coast of Australia. The letter is called *Let the Many Coastlands be Glad*. In the social justice statement they wrote that: 'The World's largest living organism, the Great Barrier Reef, is threatened with a slow death due to rising water temperature and toxic sediment run-off from the mainland.' The bishops commend the public authorities for taking steps to protect the reef. These restrict human access and reduce human pressure on the reef in order to allow it to heal itself. But they feel that greater sacrifices will have to be made by Queenslanders in order to preserve the ecological integrity of the reef. Finally the bishops call for a candid examination of lifestyle. They believe that ecological conversion means living in a more simple, sustainable and spiritual way.

Convention on Biological Diversity
The church should also support international agreements that promote awareness and action in the area of biodiversity. During the past decade and a half, concern about the destruction of species has surfaced at both the international and nation levels. In 1989 the UN organisation, United Nations Environment Programme, set up a working group to design international laws and conventions to protect biodiversity. This was in response to the current extinction spasm which is having such a devastating effect on all life forms on the planet. At the Earth Summit in Rio in 1991, 150 countries signed the Convention on Biological Diversity (CBD). By June 2004 there were 188 parties to the treaty and 168 signatures.

The objective of the CBD is to protect biodiversity and to ensure that there is a fair and equitable distribution of any financial benefits derived from these biological and genetic resources. For this reason, CBD is more in sympathy with the rights of Third World countries, traditional farmers and tribal peoples than other agreements. Articles 3 and 15 recognise the right of each country to sovereignty over its own genetic and biological resources. In order to guard against biopiracy, it requires that any person or corporation who wishes to gain access to these resources must obtain the consent of the host country (Art 15.5). This is good news for Third World countries that are rich in biological resources. It is not such good news for the pharmaceutical and agri-business corporations that would like access to these resources free of charge. The CBD is particularly mindful of the role played by tribal people and traditional farmers in enhancing and maintaining biodiversity down through the centuries (Art 8j and 15). It also affirms that 'the conservation of biological diversity is a common concern of humankind'. Article 27, 3(b) of Trade Related Intellectual Properties (TRIPs) (from the Uruguay Round of GATT) which was designed to promote the interests of transnational corporations (TNCs) effectively negates all the above provisions of the CBD. Even instruments like Plant Variety Protection (PVPs) and Material Transfer Agreements (MTAs), should be opposed by every possible means as they are merely milestones on the road to patenting all life, especially plants, by corporations and First World institutions and governments.

The 7th meeting of the Conference of Parties to the CBD took place in Kuala Lumpur from 9 to 20 February 2004. Among the priority issues addressed by the meeting were the need to protect the biological diversity of mountain ecosystems, the role of protected areas in the preservation of biological diversity, the transfer of technology between First and Third World countries to protect biodiversity, and the implementation of the targets of the 6th meeting. This set out to achieve a significant reduction in biodiversity loss by the 2010. The meeting also ratified a number of decisions pertaining to article 8j. As outlined in the previous paragraph, these relate to the respect, preservation and maintenance of knowledge, innovation and practices of indigenous people and local communities.

It is worth noting that while the US is pushing TRIPs in every possible forum, it has not yet signed the CBD or the Cartegena Protocol on Biosafety. The US Embassy in Thailand sent a strong letter to the Thai government when it began to draft legislation to protect its indigenous medical knowledge. The letter stated that the new legislation was in breach of the TRIPs agreement. Many developing countries fear that if they do not bring in TRIPs-like legislation they may be put on the United States' Super 301 'Watch List' for free-trade offenders.

People who are campaigning against TRIPS ought to promote the Convention on Biological Diversity (CBD) to ensure that there is a fair and equitable distribution of any financial benefits derived from biological and genetic resources. This is the place to design mechanisms, including financial remuneration, which will reward individuals and companies for the investment and the creativity they show in developing new products.

Ireland and Biodiversity

In April 2002, the Irish government published the National Biodiversity Plan (NBP). In an article in *WildIreland*, 'Biodiversity and the Celtic Tiger', Richard Nairn reviewed the Irish government's record on protecting biodiversity.[21] According to Nairn, if one were to judge from various papers, interdepartmental task forces and schemes like the Rural Environment protection Schemes (REPS), things look pretty good. 43,000 had signed up to REPS by the year 2000. REPS obliges farmers to limit their number of stock and reduce their use of chemical fertiliser. Farmers must also follow a farm management scheme which includes restoring hedge rows to promote biodiversity in the countryside.

Apart from the REPS programme, Nairn is not too impressed by the way Ireland has responded to the global biodiversity crisis. There has been very little financial support for farmers who wish to transform their conventional farms into organic ones. We seem to be able to find the right words in our policy documents, but effective action does not always follow. In 1992 Ireland signed the Convention on Biodiversity at the UN Conference on the Environment in Rio de Janeiro. Why did it take four years before the convention was ratified by the Irish government in 1996? Why were another six years allowed to

21. WildIreland, November-December, 2002, pages 25-27.

pass before the government produced the national biodiversity plan? Effective action is still at its infancy.

On threatened species, the NBP states that 'a review will be undertaken to determine if it would be appropriate and feasible to introduce specific legal provisions to provide for the conservation of species that might otherwise be threatened.' The drafters seem not to be aware that such an Irish Red Data Book, edited by Dr Tom Curtis, has data on vascular plants (1988), mammals, birds, amphibians and fish.

Nairn points out that there is already legal protection for rare species in the Flora Protection Order and Wildlife Act (for vertebrates). The problem is implementation. Only two species of invertebrates – the fresh water pearl mussel and the white-clawed crayfish – are protected by Statutory Instrument. There is no Red Data Book for invertebrates.

Most people know that the once common corncrake is endangered in Ireland, with only three or four habitats left. The NBP is aware of this, so Nairn asks why did the government's conservation agency, Dúchas, reverse its decision opposing planning permission for housing development along the Shannon River, in the middle of the best remaining habitat for corncrakes?

As I wrote earlier, the reason why many Irish birds are at risk is because of the intensive agriculture which is now common right around the country. NBP has no concrete strategies or programmes to address this situation. Noble sentiments will not achieve anything unless they are backed up with concrete action programmes and adequate funding. Nairn finds that not enough habitats are currently being protected in Ireland. At an EU Seminar on Atlantic Biogeographical Regions, chaired by the EU Commission in Holland in June 2002, it was found that Ireland had declared an insufficient number of protected areas for most of the habitats listed in the Habitat Directive. This is why Ireland has been condemned by the European Court of Justice for failing to adequately implement the Habitat Directive.

In July 2004 the Commission began legal proceedings against Ireland on a number of fronts. The European Court ruled in 2002 that the Irish government must take steps to reduce sheep numbers in the Owenduff-Nephin Beg complex – a 25,000 hectare area of bog and streams in County Mayo. Though actions have been taken, they are not sufficient. The Commission has complained that legal requirements to prevent habitat damage in the area have not been implemented.[22]

In a pamphlet on biodiversity in Ireland, the journalist Michael Viney points out that the official apparatus to protect habitats which are sanctioned by the EU Commission has been poorly explained and introduced to Irish people, especially those making a living in the countryside. These include National Heritage Areas (NHAs), the Special Areas of Conservation (SAC) and the Special Protection Areas (SPAs) for birds. Viney articulates what I have often heard at environmental meetings attended by farmers. 'What has the protection of snails and plants almost too small to see, or of 'ugly' parasites like lampreys (which merit no fewer than five SAC), got to do with people's real lives? They are 'threatened' or they are so 'rare': So what – who needs them, other than the scientists pursuing their own particular agenda?'[23] Setting people against other people or habitats or other species is not a good way to protect habitat. Politicians, both national and local, have engaged in such behaviour in the past few years.

Brendan Dunford's *Farming in the Burren* addresses some of these challenges and seeming contradictions in continuing with intensive, chemical agriculture that may destroy the very landscape that tourists come to see. He acknowledges that:

The upheavals of the past few decades or more in the agricultural sphere have upset the fortuitously harmonious agricultural-environment relationship that defined the

22. Denis Staunton, 'State in breach of EU environmental law', *The Irish Times*, 14 July 2004, page 8.
23. Michael Viney, *A Living Island: Ireland's responsibility to nature*, Comhar, The National Sustainable Development Partnership, Dublin, 2002, pages 12-13.

Burren and its people. Specialisation, intensification and marginalisation have occurred with farm systems of late, as farmers have struggled to reposition themselves in the shifting sands of today's global agricultural model. Increasing levels of off-farm employment and changes of ownership are also contributing to changes in management. These management changes have, in turn, resulted in significant environmental change, not least from an ecological perspective, as vegetation studies in this study have revealed.

Turning the clock back to the extensive, low-input, labour-intensive systems of old that upheld the rich diversity of the uplands is not a realistic option for the majority of Burren farmers. Instead, a new dynamic is required which will explore the common ground between the best of the old and new, in order that farmers continue to make a decent living in a way that continues to protect and enhance the landscape, while securing the invaluable heritage of the Burren for future generations.[24]

In *Why are we Deaf to the Cry of the Earth?* I argued that institutions which are presently in place, like County Councils, do not have the expertise or resources to manage an area like the Burren with its many seemingly contradictory demands. In that book, I suggested setting up a Burren Authority where all the agencies involved in the Burren would be able to work together to ensure that those living there enjoyed a decent standard of living while protecting this beautiful place for future generations.

The various agencies of the national government, in agriculture, tourism and environment, must work together to help farmers to see the long-term benefit and necessity of having special areas to protect endangered flora and fauna and habitat. One major obstacle in any planning strategy to protect Irish biodiversity is that our knowledge of many species is incomplete.

---

24. Brendan Dunford, *Farming and the Burren*, published by Teagasc, 2002, page 90.

Much of what we know is scattered in different government departments, statutory bodies, museums, universities, Coillte, Teagasc, the Central Fisheries Board, the EPA, National Parks and Wildlife Services, non-government organisations, individual collections and the like.

Michael Viney recommended the setting up of a National Biological Record Centre. This ought to be well staffed and have up-to-date and relevant computer databases to make accessing the data relatively painless. Because of the sensitive nature of the data, and the way it may be used in planning disputes, for example, Viney felt that the Centre would need to be completely independent of politicians and political influence. The reason is simple. The Centre's data will be used in environmental impact studies and planning decisions, which underline the calls for visible independence from direct government control.[25] However, concern for biodiversity must not be confined to rural Ireland. *Biodiversity in the City* published papers from an international conference held in Dublin in the autumn of 2002. One of the contributors, John Feehan, wrote, 'allowing the heart of nature to throb in the fabric of the city is not only a biological or ecological issue; it also has a geological component that nurtures body and spirit in the same way.'[26]

Michael Viney's hope for a Centre free from political interference and patronage will be hard to realise in Ireland. The Minister for the Environment announced the setting up of the National Biological Records Centre (NBRC) on 25 March 2004. In the speech where he announced his plans he said: 'I'm aware that several academic institutions are very interested in hosting the centre and I expect to be able to announce the location in the near future.'[27] In early July, it emerged that no other academic institution had been approached before a statement was released by the Waterford Institute of Technology on 29 June 2004

25. Michael Viney, 'Keeping stock of our natural environment', *The Irish Times*, 14 June 2003, page 9 (Weekend Review).
26. Quoted in Michael Viney's 'Finding space in suburban sprawl'.
27. Sam Smyth, 'Row looms over Minister's hometown move', *Irish Independent*, 7 July 2004, page 12.

saying that it was confident that the NBRC would be located on
their campus. As Sam Smyth of the *Irish Independent* wrote, this
is the Minister's hometown. Putting political considerations before competence and experience is not a very auspicious way to
begin such an important agency. Desmond Crofton, a senior
member of the Heritage Council's wildlife committee, resigned
in protest at what he described as the Minister's 'political
stroke'.[28] Crofton claimed that this decision was in contraven-
tion of the requirement that all public contracts above 50,000
euro must be put up for tender publicly. The annual running
costs of the NBRC will be in the region of 600,000 euro.
Spokespersons for both the Heritage Council and the Department of the Environment deny any political interference or patronage. Most conveniently, the Minister made the announcement just as the Dáil was rising in the summer of 2004. He will
not have to answer questions on the issue in the Dáil until late
September 2004.

The National Monuments Act which the Minister for the
Environment rushed through the Oireachtas before the summer
recess of 2004 is 'ill considered and hastily drafted', according to
Maighreád Mc Parland, the Honorary Secretary of the Institute
for the Conservation of Historic and Artistic Works in Ireland.
She argues that the 'effect of the act is to facilitate the destruction
of our heritage, unlike previous National Monuments acts in
which protection and conservation were the guiding principles
… The impetus for the new act seems to have come from the
Minister's desire to favour development at the expense of heritage.'[29] If we continue to destroy our environment and heritage
and treat them as political footballs, we will certainly endanger
our tourist industry. Visitors do not come to Ireland to bask in
the sun. They come to see our varied and beautiful environments. They come to the Burren for its spectacular beauty and its
flora and fauna. These include spring gentians, mountain avens,

---

28. Ibid.
29. 'National Monuments Act', letter to *The Irish Times*, 27 August 2004,
page 19.

ladies bedstraw, bloody crane's bill, the golden carline thistle, grass of Parnassus and an array of orchids. If these disappear and are replaced by second homes, with their tonsured lawns, fields of ryegrass and knapweed, visitors will not return to the Burren. Neither will they go to Kerry, West Clare or Connemara to see plantations of sitka spruce. Given the importance of tourism to our economy, it is surprising that Ireland occupied the lowest place in the tables of the World Conservation Union in the proportion of the country which is given full national park protection. Only 1% of the country is fully protected, as against 12% in over 30 First World countries.[30]

Little has been done to make agriculture more ecologically friendly. Much of the farm subsidy regime, especially headage payment, has done terrible damage to a variety of vegetation, especially heather, on Irish hills and mountains in the west of Ireland. This was a classic example of a well-intentioned social policy having a disastrous ecological consequence. The EU initiative offered a subsidy on ewes to encourage lamb production by small farmers in 'disadvantaged areas'. It resulted in the near destruction of blanket bog vegetation on mountains in the west of Ireland.

NBP states that Ireland holds 8% of the world's blanket bog. It suggests that significant work is being done to protect this habitat. Nairn points to the fact that at All Saints Bog in Co Offaly two-thirds of the bog is state-owned but 'the remainder is being mined for peat moss. The result is that the whole bog is drying out and is unlikely to survive.'[31] Patrick Crushell, the conservation officer with the Irish Peatland Conservation Council (IPCC), agrees with Nairn.[32]

There are a few rays of hope regarding bog rehabilitation. Coillte is running a 4.2 million euro project which aims to bring 14 bogs back to life. The research programme began in 2002 and,

30. Michael Viney, op. cit., page 14-15. *The Irish Times*, 31 May 2003, page 9.
31. Richard Nairn, op. cit., page 27.
32. Patrick Crushell, 'Inertia on Conservation', letter to *The Irish Times*, 6 March 2001.

according to the ecological consultant Dr John Conaghan, is 'all very experimental. It is the first time that this has been done here (in Ireland).'[33] 1,200 hectares of blanket bog, mainly in the west of Ireland, are involved in this project. The rehabilitation is being carried out in co-operation with the EU's Life-Nature programme which aims to conserve Europe's flora and fauna. Unfortunately, bog rehabilitation does not encompass the huge midland bogs run by Bórd na Móna.

Another project, entitled Ag-biota, is a 5-year study of plants, insects and birds on Irish agricultural lands. Over 20 scientists from major Third Level Institutes in the country, from UCD to the University of Limerick and Teagasc, are involved in the study. Already they have found 85 new species of wasps on 10 intensive farms. Maybe 10 times that amount will found on less intensively managed farms.[34]

In summary, Nairn thinks that the National Biodiversity Plan is big on promises and short on performance. He feels that the cutbacks announced in all Departments in 2003 will adversely affect the ability of state agencies to protect Ireland's biodiversity. NBP estimates that an extra 14 staff members needs to be appointed and 38.6 million euro put in place to implement the proposals in the document. Nairn thought that the transfer of Dúchas to the Department of Environment and Local Government was a positive move. This means that 'nature conservation is now the responsibility of the same minister who deals with physical planning and the local authorities.'

Then came the bombshell in April 2003 with the announcement that Dúchas was being abolished and the staff was being distributed to the Department of the Environment and the Office of Public Works (OPW). A Dúchas staff member told Eileen Battersby of The Irish Times that 'archaeology is seen as too expensive in terms of time and money for developers. By

33. Dick Ahlstrom, 'Bringing our ailing bogs back to life', The Irish Times, 8 July 2004, page 19.
34. Michael Viney, 'Shining a light on world of wasps', The Irish Times, 7 August 2004, page3.

placing heritage within the Department of the Environment, the very department involved with planning, the heritage function is compromised, says a Dúchas staff member who declined to be named.'[35] Archaeologists and environmentalists fear that, within the Department of the Environment, Ireland's archaeological and architectural heritage will be emasculated. It is well known that the pro-building section of the government, especially capital projects like road building, felt frustrated by the activities of Dúchas and lobbied for its demise. That the Minister for the Environment succumbed to this pressure does not augur well for the protection of the wider environment when short-term economic arguments win out over the long-term protection of our heritage.

Opposition politicians question whether the Minister had the power to initiate such a drastic change on an administrative basis, rather than in the context of two forthcoming Bills dealing with heritage-related matters.[36]

In a second editorial in *The Irish Times*, entitled 'End of Dúchas', the editor reviewed the ups-and-downs of Dúchas over the past number of years. Dúchas annoyed the European Commission by not being aggressive enough about identifying areas for conservation. It's stocking policy drew fire from farmers and its conservation approach annoyed 'developers'. Nevertheless it made quality brochures available on our landscape to citizens and tourists. In the judgement of the editor 'Dúchas delivered as an integrated heritage agency. It should be retained.'[37]

There is a wide-ranging NGO community interested in different dimensions of biodiversity in Ireland. Some operate at the national level, others like Save Our Lough Derg (SOLD) at local level. Irish citizens must rally behind the recent call by a coali-

---

35. Eileen Battersby, 'Knocking down Dúchas', *The Irish Times*, 19 April 2003, page 4, Weekend Review.
36. Frank McDonald, 'Break-up of Dúchas "maybe unlawful"', *The Irish Times*, 23 April 2003, page 4.
37. Editorial in *The Irish Times*, 28 April 2002, page 17.

tion of environmental organisations like VOICE, EarthWatch, An Taisce, BirdWatch Ireland, Crann, CoastWatch and the Irish Peatland Conservation Council, for more stringent protection for the Irish environment. Unfortunately these organisations are very poorly funded, are not well supported financially by the public, and have little enough access to the media. This is in comparison to other European countries where environmental organisations are well supported.

One NGO deserves a special mention in any Irish book on conserving indigenous biodiversity. It is called the Irish Seed Savers Association (ISSA) which is located in Capparoe, Scarrif, Co Clare. This organisation specialises in locating and preserving traditional varieties of fruits, cereals, grasses and vegetables. Since the early 1990s ISSA have found over 140 varieties of Irish apple trees. They have located long lost Irish grains from places like Norway and Russia. They now have 25 native Irish varieties of oats, and several varieties of wheat, barely and rye. On their property in east Clare, ISSA has two plots devoted to Irish native trees. ISSA has passed on these trees and cereals to gardeners so that the Irish genetic heritage may continue to flourish.[38] May their tribe increase.

Offaly Biodiversity Strategy
Another hopeful sign, in an otherwise bleak horizon, is the development of biodiversity strategy at local level. The biologist, Dr John Feehan, in an inaugural lecture in June 2004, outlined what might be involved in the biodiversity strategy for a county like Offaly. First of all it calls for the setting up of a scientific steering group. Each individual on the group, apart from bringing energy and commitment to the project, would also be able to avail of resources and expertise which can be found presently within their own organisation, for example, Coillte or the National Parks and Wildlife Service. Secondly, they are attempting to assemble a taxonomy panel. Scientists on that panel will advise the group about the status and conservation needs of

---

38. Email address for ISSA: issa@esatclear.ie

their particular speciality. This panel will play a key role in spelling out the research agenda and the actions that need to be taken to protect or enhance a species in the area. It is hoped that a State of the Wild in Offaly Report will be ready in 2005. The panel will also identify biological hotspots in the country.

Thus far people might feel that biodiversity is the exclusive domain of scientists. The Offaly group want to dispel this myth and democratise the process in an effort to involve every individual and the various communities and groups within the county. Among these are environmental organisations and civic groups, local authorities personnel, and believers from the various churches. An Annual Biodiversity Summer School for Teachers in Offaly will be held each July in an effort to involve primary teachers and those in secondary school who teach science or religion. In contrast to local biodiversity plans in Britain, for example, which lack any ethical or religious underpinning for protecting or enhancing biodiversity, the Offaly Biodiversity Strategy hopes to have a strong ethical, religious and aesthetic dimension to the programme.

In order to increase awareness of the importance of biodiversity and promote the Offaly Biodiversity Strategy, prominent Offaly people from a variety of backgrounds – sporting or religious – will be asked to endorse the programme. Posters with such endorsements will be displayed in schools, churches, pubs and other public places.

The churches should support such initiatives and other organisations which educate people about the importance of biodiversity at national and international level. Names like the World Wide Fund For Nature (WWF) and the World Conservation Union spring to mind. Initiatives like the Forest Stewardship Council (FSC) that attempt to regulate trade in forest products deserve the wholehearted backing of Christians, as does the work of the Convention on International Trade in Endangered Species (CITES). Individuals can help promote forestry that is both sustainable and socially just by demanding that the timber items they purchase have been certified by the

Forest Stewardship Council (FSC).[39] By the end of 2002 the FSC had certified 30 million hectares of forest globally as managed in a sustainable way. While Coillte's (Irish Forest Service) application for FSC certification was approved in 2002 a number of Irish environmental organisations, like VOICE, opposed the FSC certification, because of Coillte's bias towards conifers. The certification only requires that 10% of their planting be broadleaf. Anglers complain that conifers planted right up to the bank of rivers have increased their acidity thus killing off aquatic invertebrates which fish eat. Many formerly fine trout and salmon rivers are now almost dead and devoid of fish.[40] The Heritage Council in Ireland has recommended a 50:50 ration of conifers to broadleaves, while groups like VOICE are campaigning for 50% plus broadleaves.[41]

Promoting a New, Sustainable Culture
International institutions must promote and facilitate sustainability. At the moment there is no legal mechanism that allows a country to block the importation of timber that has been cut illegally. In fact the World Trade Organisation now works in favour of the exploiter, despite the fact that the public was promised greener and more just policies at Doha in 2002.[42]

During the past decade, billions of pounds have been spent by corporations, universities and states researching and promoting recombinant DNA technologies. Some of the genetically engineered plants, animals and fish are already being marketed commercially. Many critics claim that these genetically-engineered organisms are harmful to human health, destructive towards the environment, and socially divisive .[43]

At the moment the jury is out on that debate, but it surely should not be out on the contention that much more political

39. Janet, N. Abramovitz, op. cit., page 53.
40. Michael Viney, *A Living Island: Ireland's responsibility to nature*, Comhar, The National Sustainable Partnership, Dublin, 2003, page 13.
41. www. voice.buz.org/forestry/index.html 19/04/03 page 1.
42. Ibid., page 64.
43. Seán McDonagh, *Patenting Life? Stop!*, Dominican Publications, Dublin, 2003.

will and financial resources ought to be committed to protecting habitats for species that are threatened with extinction. In a lecture delivered on 2 May 2001 at the National Science Foundation in Arlington, Virginia, USA, Professor Edward Wilson stated that it would only take $28 billion to permanently save 70% of the known plant and animal species in the world. When one thinks of the fact that the global military budget reaches over $1,000 billion per year it beggars the imagination that it is so difficult to come by the paltry sum of $28 billion to prevent the biological impoverishment of the planet.

The money could be used in a variety of ways. One initiative would be to buy access to the world's most important and threatened areas, especially in the Congo, New Guinea, the Amazon and other biodiversity 'hotspots' around the world.[44] In *The Future of Life*, Professor Wilson added the Philippines, Indo-Burma, and India as well as the Mediterranean-climate scrublands of South Africa, South western Australia, and southern California to his list.[45] We also need to define the marine hotspots and to give them the same protection. This calls for money to speed up mapping the world's biological diversity. Money must also be made available to rehabilitate devastated ecosystems before it is too late. In the Philippines money, resources and training is needed to promote reforestation projects using indigenous trees. The same is true of coral reefs and mangrove forests.

Some of this money should also be made available to tribal people and those who live in forest areas to manage their habitat in a sustainable way. Someone like myself, who spent over a decade living close to tropical rainforests, knows that combating poverty and promoting fairness and equity is an essential ingredient in protecting the natural habitat.

Edward Wilson would like to see biodiversity used to im-

44. Forest Conservation News Today, *Biodiversity Endgame: Buy Conservation of Endangered Ecosystems*, Forest Network a Project of Forest.org, Inc., May 5, 2001.
45. Edward O. Wilson, op.cit., page 160.

prove the global economy. This would mean encouraging more research so that plants, animals and other creatures might benefit people, especially the poor.[46] I would support such a suggestion as long as public bodies rather than corporations promote this research. The corporate world is so focused on the bottom line profit that it is naïve to think that they will promote biodiversity or anything else for its own sake. Wilson recognises this when he proposes that 'the private sector, working within the public-trust constraints defined by government policy, is the engine of society'.[47] Non-government organisations like Greenpeace, Friends of the Earth, the Sierra Club, the WorldWide Fund for Nature, Conservation International, International Union for the Conservation of Nature (IUCN) and other local biodiversity groups have played a central role in educating the public, politicians and even the private sector on the importance of environmental issues. IUCN publishes a Red Data List to draw attention to species that are threatened with extinction, in order to alert governments and other NGOs so that some action can be taken to protect the species before it is too late. Due, however, to lack of funds, personnel and knowledge of lesser known species, it is impossible to report with any degree of accuracy on any but the most well known wild species.[48]

World Bank

Some people might argue that the World Bank would be the appropriate institution to manage such a fund and promote the research. Unfortunately the Bank's record in tropical forestry matters has been so dismal that they ought not to be the main agency tasked with administering this fund. The World Bank funded massive projects that directly destroyed huge areas of tropical forest. In *Mortgaging the Earth*, Bruce Rich examined a number of these projects which turned out to be social and environmental disasters. Two Brazilian projects (a mining,

---

46. Ibid., page 163.
47. Ibid., page 165.
48. R. F. Dasmann, *Planet in Peril?: Man and the Biosphere Today*, Penguin Books, London, 1972, page 110.

smelting and railway development) and Polonoroeste (road building and agricultural colonisation) were particularly destructive. Despite the historical fact that previous efforts to colonise the Amazon had failed dismally, and the advice of the Bank's own Operations Evaluation Department (OED) which had raised serious doubts about the viability of the project, hundreds of millions of dollars were poured into the Polonoroeste project in the 1980s. Rich wrote that Polonoroeste 'transformed Rodonia – an area approximately the size of Oregon or Great Britain – into a region with one of the highest forest destruction rates in the Brazilian Amazon'.[49]

The Carajas project had a similar impact on the tropical forest at the other end of the Amazon basin in the state of Para. Here the World Bank lent over £300 million to build a railway to transport high-grade ore to the sea. Included in the original project were plans to build 34 charcoal-burning industries to produce pig iron along the railway corridor. Timber for charcoal was supposed to come from eucalyptus plantations. In fact it came from the standing forests and this has resulted in massive deforestation in the area.

Another area where the World Bank has a serious test of ecological stewardship is in the way it handled Third World Debt in the 1980s and 1990s. It seldom pointed out how debt repayments have increased tropical forest destruction. In Brazil the Amazon forest has been burnt each year to facilitate beef production which is destined for global fast-foods outlets, supposedly to get foreign exchange with which to repay its massive debts. In Guyana most of the forest that covers 70% of the country has been sold off in an effort to raise foreign currency to pay the foreign debt. The economist Susan George reproduced a chart showing that the majority of the top debtor countries, like Brazil and Mexico, had increased their levels of deforestation significantly in the 1970s and 1980s. The increase in Brazil was by a whopping 245%.[50]

---

49. Bruce Rich, *Mortgaging the Earth: The World Bank, Environmental Impoverishment and the Crisis of Development*, Beacon Press, Boston, 1994, page 26.

The Bank also funded the ecologically and culturally disastrous transmigration programme in Indonesia. In other tropical areas like the Philippines, the widespread poverty which has followed in the wake of SAPs has driven millions of poor landless people into the rainforests in search of land on which to eke out an existence. In *The Greening of the Church*, I criticised the conditions imposed on debtor countries by the Structural Adjustment Programmes of both the World Bank and the International Monetary Fund, on the grounds that they promoted deforestation and stopped national governments from investing in protecting their forests. Programmes that supported the training of forest guards and good natural resource planning were cut from the national budget.[51] Paul Brown stated, in an article in the *Guardian Weekly*, that a study showed that multinational corporations had bribed and bullied their way into the international logging trade, and that the IMF and World Bank were also guilty of 'inducing countries to sell their forests for a quick cash return to pay off debts to western countries'.[52] The report that carried this critical information was suppressed by the European Commission and the World Wide Fund for Nature for three years.

Nevertheless, financial institutions like the World Bank, International Monetary Fund and other multilateral financial institutions should make a huge contribution to the Forest Survival Fund and request First World governments to do likewise. This survival fund might be linked to an agency like the United Nations Environment and Development Agency (UNDP).

While multilateral funding is crucial for the success of initiatives to protect biodiversity hotspots, the World Bank and the International Monetary Fund (IMF) need to change their model of development. For the past 20 years, but particularly in the

50. Susan George, *The Debt Boomerang*, Pluto Press, London, 1992, pages 8 and 9.
51. Seán McDonagh, *The Greening of the Church*, Geoffrey Chapman, 1990, pages 9-37.
52. Paul Brown, 'Report on Forest Suppressed', *The Guardian Weekly*, 1 June 2000, page 3.

1990s, they have been promoting free trade, export-oriented crops and industry and forcing countries to open their markets to competition. The impact of such policies on many Third World countries has been disastrous. After trade liberalisation, growth rates in Ghana and Zambia fell as many industries could not cope with foreign competition. 54 countries, many in Africa, are now poorer than they were in 1990 as a result of these policies.[53] The price of maize has fallen by one third in the Philippines since it opened its markets to exports in 1997. This was mainly because cheap US corn flooded the market. US farmers on average receive $20,000 a year in subsidies while poor corn farmers in Mindanao have to live on $365 a year.[54] Countries are no longer planting their staple food, like rice, corn, root crops and vegetables. They are being forced into producing cash crops for export. The staple food for many Third World countries will in future be grown in the US, Europe and Australia. Such policies are not sustainable. They are also very dangerous from the point of view of food security. As transport costs increase in the next decade, many countries that are no longer growing their own food will experience hunger and famine and probably political pressure from First World countries who are now growing their staple food.

Conclusion

In this book I have attempted to look at what is happening to life on our planet today. It is clear that species are being lost at a totally unprecedented pace. Unless we change and protect life, and particular habitats, one third to one half of the species of the world will be lost in a mere 45 years.

Unfortunately, the Christian churches have been slow to recognise the attack on life which is so relentless today. Many Christian churches claim to be pro-life. In fact what they mean is that they are opposed to abortion. But a truly pro-life stance

---

53. Devinder Sharma, 'Hungry for Trade: The Statue of Liberty is crying, July 18, 2004', *Zed Commentary*, <sysop@zmag.org>, printed 20 July 2004, page 2.
54. Ibid.

would address what is happening to life in every part of the world, especially in rich ecosystems like coral reefs and tropical forests. Such a truly pro-life approach would enhance the various Christian churches' opposition to abortion.

The churches should support every initiative to promote biodiversity, and spearhead an awareness programme in order to educate the public, and especially the political and commercial leaders, so that decisive action is taken soon. Church related development agencies like Trócaire (in Ireland) and Cafod (in England and Wales) must a take much more pro-active approach in campaigning to protect biodiversity in countries where they work in partnership with local church-based non-government organisations. Money, educational opportunities, and communications technologies need to be made available, especially in Third World countries, to train competent people, among them botanists, biologists and zoologists, to form the nucleus of task forces designed to stem the haemorrhage of extinction before it is too late. Catholic universities and colleges ought to be in the forefront of such endeavours, and regular bulletins should be available in the Catholic media tracking endangered species and supporting a variety of remedial strategies.

Local churches ought to set aside one day each year to celebrate the gift of all life on earth. A devotion to Jesus Prince or Author of Life and liturgies devised for such a feast would help educate Catholics about the crucial importance of all living species. We should not forget humans will only thrive in a world where biodiversity is respected and actively promoted.

Human Vocation

Within the perspective of the new cosmology, our unique human vocation is to celebrate the beauty and fruitfulness of all life on Earth. All life has a common ancestor. All species today share basic molecular traits. Tissue is divided into cells. The genetic information is stored in DNA; it is transcribed into RNA, and than translated into proteins. Finally, a large array of mostly similar proteins catalyst, the enzymes, accelerate all life processes.[55] In the human species the earth and all the cosmos has become aware of itself in the thoughts, feeling and imagination of individual human beings. This means that we must quickly grow out of the destructive adolescent phase of our development, which now threatens to destroy or degrade everything from our precious air to the creatures who live with us on the Earth and in the seas, and begin to actively care for God's creation.

Both as human beings and as Christians we are challenged to come to know, in a much more intimate way, the natural world around us. This is, after all, God's creation. Only if we know it will we be able to celebrate and promote this love of life in the face of the culture of violence and death which is so prevalent in our times. Protecting life ought surely to be the vocation of every Christian today.

Each generation of humans has its own particular task to accomplish. In the early part of the 19th century, it involved working to abolish slavery. Later in the 19th century, the focus moved to protecting workers' rights. These were momentous changes in human history but they could have come at a different point in time. The challenge facing this generation is quite different. It is one that has never faced a generation of humans in the past and never will be faced by a future generation of humans. This is the mass extinction of other creatures in just a few short decades. The task quite simply is to take decisive action to stave off the extinction of species which could sterilise the planet. If this generation does not act, no future generation will be able to undo the damage that this generation has caused to the planet. It is an extraordinary and awesome moment that the behaviour of a single generation of humans can have such a profound and irreversible impact, not just on human history, but on the life of the planet as well. Lastly, species extinction cannot continue with impunity. Sooner or later, extinction will rob our planet of the ability to sustain many forms of life, possibly even our own.

Life on planet earth has developed and diversified during

55. Edward O. Wilson, *The Future of Life*, op. cit., page 132.

the past 3.8 billion years. Living forms moved into almost every nook and cranny on the planet. Humans had nothing to do with this florescence and we are one of the most recent arrivals at the table of life. Now the evolutionary future of the planet is quite simply in the hands of this generation.